PATTON

PATTON

BLOOD, GUTS, AND PRAYER

MICHAEL KEANE

REGNERY
HISTORY

Cataloging-in-Publication data on file with the Library of Congress
ISBN 978-1-59698-326-7

Published in the United States by
Regnery Publishing, Inc.
One Massachusetts Avenue NW
Washington, DC 20001
www.RegneryHistory.com

Manufactured in the United States of America
10 9 8 7 6 5 4 3 2 1

Books are available in quantity for promotional or premium use. Write to Director of Special Sales, Regnery Publishing, Inc., One Massachusetts Avenue NW, Washington, DC 20001, for information on discounts and terms, or call (202) 216-0600.

Distributed to the trade by
Perseus Distribution
250 West 57th Street
New York, NY 10107

For my parents—
My father, Al, who taught me about Patton.
My mother, Peggy, who taught me about prayer.

"The bravest are the tenderest. The loving are the daring."

—BAYARD TAYLOR

CONTENTS

APPENDICES

GEORGE S. PATTON JR.

TIMELINE

1885 November 11	Patton was born in San Gabriel, Los Angeles County, California.
1897–1903	Patton attended Stephen Cutter Clark's Classical School for Boys, Pasadena, California.
1903–1904	Patton attended Virginia Military Institute, Lexington, Virginia, as Cadet.
1904 June 16	Patton entered U.S. Military Academy, West Point, New York.
1905 June 5	Patton turned back to repeat initial year.

September 1	Patton re-entered as Cadet, U.S. Military Academy.
1909 June 11	Patton was promoted to the rank of second lieutenant, 15th Cavalry.
September 12	Patton joined 15th Cavalry, Fort Sheridan, Illinois, and was assigned to Troop K.
1910 May 26	Patton and Beatrice Banning Ayer were married; they would later have three children.
1911 March 19	Patton's first child, Beatrice Ayer, was born.
1912 June 14	Patton sailed for Europe to participate in the Olympic Games in Stockholm, Sweden.
July 7	Patton participated in Modern Pentathlon, Olympic Games.
July–August	Patton received individual instruction in fencing at Saumur, France.
1915 February 28	Patton's second child, Ruth Ellen Patton, was born.
1916 March 13	Patton detached from 8th Cavalry and attached to headquarters, Punitive Expedition, Mexico.
May 14	Patton led soldiers who engaged Pancho Villa's bodyguard and others at Rubio Ranch.
May 23	Patton was promoted to the rank of first lieutenant.

1917 May 15	Patton was promoted to the rank of captain.
May 18	Patton was ordered to report to General Pershing in Washington, D.C.; appointed Commanding Officer, Headquarters Troop, AEF.
November 10	Detailed to the Tank Service.
1918 January 26	Patton was promoted to the temporary rank of major.
March 23	Patton, as commanding officer of the American Tank School in France, received his first 10 light tanks by train.
March 30	Patton was promoted to the temporary rank of lieutenant colonel.
September 15	St. Mihiel Offensive was launched.
September 26	Patton was seriously wounded during the Meuse-Argonne Offensive in France.
October 17	Patton was promoted to the temporary rank of colonel.
December 16	Patton was awarded the Distinguished Service Cross.
1920 June 20	Patton reverted to the permanent rank of captain.
July 1	Patton was promoted to the permanent rank of major.

October 3	Patton joined 3d Cavalry at Fort Myer, Virginia, as Commanding Officer, 3d Squadron.
1923 December 24	Patton's son, George Patton IV, was born.
1924 July 30	Patton was an Honor Graduate, Command and General Staff College.
1925 March 4	Patton sailed from New York to Hawaii on the Army Transport ship Chateau-Thierry going through the Panama Canal.
March 31	Reached Hawaii and was assigned to the G-1 and G-2 Hawaiian Division.
1927 June	Patton's father, George Smith Patton, died.
1928 October 6	Patton's mother, Ruth Wilson Patton, died.
1932 June 2	Patton was awarded the Purple Heart for a wound sustained in 1918.
June 11	Became Distinguished Graduate, Army War College.
1934 March 1	Patton was promoted to the permanent rank of lieutenant colonel.
1935 May 7	Patton departed Los Angeles for Hawaii.
June 8	Arrived in Honolulu and was assigned to G-2, Hawaiian Department.
1937 June 12	Patton departed Honolulu.
July 12	Arrived in Los Angeles.

July 25	Spent time in Beverly, Massachusetts hospital with a broken leg.
November 14	Discharged from the hospital, sick in quarters.
1938 July 1	Patton was promoted to the permanent rank of colonel.
July 24	Patton served as Commanding Officer, 5th Cavalry, Fort Clark, Texas.
December 10	Patton served as Commanding Officer, 3d Cavalry, Fort Myer, Virginia.
1940 April 1	Served as Umpire, Spring Maneuvers, Fort Benning, Georgia.
May 1	Served as Control Officer, Maneuvers, Fort Beauregard, Louisiana.
October 2	Patton was promoted to the temporary rank of brigadier general.
July 26	Patton served as Commanding Officer, 2d Armored Brigade of 2d Armored Division, Fort Benning.
1941 April 4	Patton was promoted to the temporary rank of major general.
April 11	Patton was made the commanding officer of the 2nd Armored Division.
1943 March 6	Patton was named the commanding officer of the US II Corps.

March 12	Patton was promoted to the temporary rank of lieutenant general.
July 15	Patton formed a provisional corps in western Sicily, Italy.
August 3	Patton visited a field hospital in Sicily, Italy, and slapped Charles Kuhl for what he considered cowardice as Kuhl suffered no physical wounds.
August 10	Patton visited the 93rd Evacuation Hospital in Sicily, Italy, and berated Private Paul Bennett for cowardice.
November 21	Journalist Drew Pearson publicized George Patton's "slapping incident" of Aug 3, 1943.
1944 July 6	Patton secretly flew into Normandy, France, while the Germans still believed he would lead the main invading force at Pas de Calais.
August 16	Patton was promoted to the permanent rank of major general, bypassing the permanent rank of brigadier general.
December 8	Patton calls Chaplain James H. O'Neill and asks if he has "a good prayer for weather."
December 12–14	Prayer cards are distributed to Patton's troops, asking, "Grant us fair weather for battle."
December 16	Germany launched offensive in the Ardennes known as the Battle of the Bulge.
December 20	Weather in the Ardennes cleared.

1945 March 17	Eisenhower ordered Patton to cease making plans to enter German-occupied Czechoslovakia.
March 24	Patton urinated into the Rhine River. Upon completing his crossing over a pontoon bridge, he took some dirt on the far bank, emulating his favorite historical figure William the Conqueror.
March 26	Task Force Baum heads out for Hammelburg to liberate the prisoner of war camp there. One of the prisoners is Patton's son-in-law, John K. Waters.
April 14	Patton was promoted to the permanent rank of general.
May 12	Patton launched Operation Cowboy in Hostau, Czechoslovakia, rescuing 1,200 horses, including 375 of the Lipizzan breed, from potential Soviet slaughter.
June 9	Patton and James Doolittle were honored at a parade in Los Angeles, California.
June 10	Patton addressed a crowd of 100,000 civilians in Burbank, California.
September 22	Taken out of context, Patton's careless comparison of Nazi Party members in Germany to Democratic Party or Republican Party members in the United States stirred much controversy.
October 2	Patton was relieved for statements made to the press about former Nazi Party members.

December 9	Patton sustained spinal cord and neck injuries in an automobile accident near Neckarstadt, Germany.
December 21	Patton passed away from pulmonary embolism as the result of an automobile accident.
1946 March 19	Patton's remains were moved to a different gravesite within the Luxembourg American Cemetery and Memorial in Hamm, Luxembourg.
1953 September 30	Patton's widow, Beatrice, died of a ruptured aortic aneurysm while horseback riding at Hamilton, Massachusetts. Her ashes were later strewn over her husband's grave.

PROLOGUE

September 26, 1918

Lieutenant Colonel George S. Patton Jr. lay dying in a shallow bomb crater somewhere in "No Man's Land," the deadly area dividing the German and American lines near the village of Cheppy in Lorraine. Minutes earlier, an enemy machine gun bullet had torn through his body, entering his groin and exiting his buttocks, ripping open a wound the size of a teacup. Between the bursts of machine gun fire Patton could hear the excited conversations of German soldiers who had just taken up a position in a trench a mere forty yards away. It was useless to try to move from the relative safety of the small hollow blown in the earth.

Patton was thirty-two years old. As blood poured from his wound, he serenely contemplated his own death. It was not a terrible thing, he thought. In fact, it was surprisingly easy. According to St. Paul, "The last enemy that shall be destroyed is death." More accurately, reflected Patton, the last enemy that shall be destroyed is *fear of* death.[1]

Lying in a bomb crater, surrounded by the horrors of war, Patton was overwhelmed by a deep feeling of warmth and peace, comfort and love. He realized how profoundly death was related to life, how unimportant the change from life to death really was, how everlasting the soul. He felt that love was all around him, like a subdued light.[2] He had now achieved his destiny, joining the legions of ancestors before him. *Blood.* He had not failed them; he had shown his courage and faced his fears. *Guts.* He was dying; but he had no fear of death. He was comforted by his unshakeable faith, a faith he had held since childhood and that he had carefully nurtured every day since. *Prayer.*

This is the story of George S. Patton Jr.—a story that cannot be properly told or understood without chronicling the history of one man's blood, guts, and prayer.

PART I

BLOOD

George S. Patton Jr. venerated his warrior forbears with an obsession that bordered on ancestor worship. He saw himself not as an individual but as the latest in a line of fallen heroes. He was inspired by the pantheon of forefathers who had bravely served as soldiers before him. He would frequently visit their battlefields and cemeteries, seeking to channel their bravery. As his grandson wrote:

> It would become Georgie's lifelong habit to conjure reveries and mystical moments while wandering cemeteries, old battlefields, and ancient ruins—preferably at night, alone. It was part of his search for connection to the past. The romance of death attracted him. It was eerie, magical, dangerous. It made him feel alive.[1]

Patton himself confessed that he felt a "strange fascination" in exploring old battlefields. He described in moving terms a visit to the Gettysburg battlefield, where two of his relatives had been killed:

> To get in the proper frame of mind I wandered through the cemetery and let the spirits of the dead thousands laid there in ordered rows sink deep into me. Then just as the sun sank behind South Mountain I walked down to the scene of Pickett's great charge and, seated on a rock just where Olmstead and two of my great uncles died, I watched the wonder of the day go out.... It was very wonderful and no one came to bother me.[2]

Before his admission to West Point, Patton entered the Virginia Military Institute, which his father and paternal grandfather had both attended. After VMI, Patton's father chose a career in business and politics rather than the military. He later shared a secret with his son, admitting that he was "a man of peace." Perhaps Papa Patton had witnessed too much carnage during the American Civil War. Nevertheless, the father infused his son with romantic notions of war that would fuel his military ambitions, and the father's political connections in southern California secured the future general's admission to West Point.

CHAPTER ONE

GHOSTS OF THE CONFEDERACY

WALLER TAZEWELL PATTON
GEORGE SMITH PATTON
HUGH MERCER

*"I am crying because I have only seven sons
left to fight the Yankees."*

—PEGGY PATTON

The train pulled into the station at Winchester, Virginia, hours late, having been delayed at several stops along the route from Baltimore. Dark had fallen and a steady rain pelted the roof of the railcar. Inside the dark baggage car, the teenage Virginia Military Institute cadet sat on top of the casket containing his uncle, a fallen Civil War veteran. As the heavy metal doors of the railcar rumbled open, they revealed a tight huddle of men collected on the train platform, the flickering light from their lanterns reflecting off their rain-soaked oilskin ponchos. The cadet moved nervously toward the open door. If the transfer of the body had not been properly cleared, he might face arrest.

"Who are you?" he asked the men gathered outside the railcar. "What do you want?"

One of the dark figures stepped forward and unbuttoned his poncho, revealing the dress uniform of a Confederate army officer. The men silently boarded the train and carried the casket of the fallen hero to a mule-drawn wagon. The dark figures followed the casket as it slowly made its way to the cemetery, accompanied by an elderly veteran beating a muffled drum and a flag bearer holding the outlawed Stars and Bars of the defeated rebellion of Southern states.

Inside the cemetery, the casket was brought alongside a trench that had been cleared for its burial, next to the site of the cadet's father, also a fallen Civil War hero and the brother of the dead man whom the cadet had escorted from Baltimore. But the trench, it turned out, was too small. Grabbing a shovel, the young man lowered himself into the hole to widen it. He glanced at his father's exposed casket. After ten years in the ground, the wooden planks had rotted away, and by the eerie, flickering lantern light he could see the face, the long beard, and, at the throat, the gold brocade of his father's gray uniform. Years later the son, George Smith Patton II, would comment simply about the sight of his father's cadaver, "He looked exactly as I remembered him."

The uncle whose casket was interred next to that of George Smith Patton I was Waller Tazewell Patton, named for a governor of Virginia, Littleton Waller Tazewell. Called Tazewell or "Taz" by his family, he was one of twelve children of John Mercer Patton and his wife, Peggy. Of the nine children who survived infancy, eight were sons, and Taz was the youngest. At the outbreak of the Civil War, Tazewell enlisted in the Confederate army, eventually achieving the rank of lieutenant colonel and taking command of the Seventh Virginia Infantry. He was badly wounded at the second battle of Manassas on August 30, 1862, and was sent home to recuperate from a bullet hole through his right hand. His family could not help but notice how the bloody experience of battle over the past year had transformed

Tazewell from a boisterous and flippant youth into a spiritual man who spoke often of religion and reflected upon his desire to lead a pure and holy life. He seemed haunted by the violence and killing of which he had been a part.

While he recovered, Tazewell was elected to the Virginia Senate. He could have honorably resigned his military commission to serve as a full-time legislator, but he chose instead to return to his outfit, which in December 1862 was assigned to the division of General George Pickett in Robert E. Lee's Army of Northern Virginia. Tazewell would be severely wounded during Pickett's famous charge, the failed frontal assault on the Union's heavily defended battle line on the third and final day of the battle of Gettysburg. Crossing nearly a mile of open field in a deliberate march, the rebel troops were battered by the Union guns. It was a horrifying spectacle of violence which the soldiers on both sides would remember with reverence and awe until their dying moments. Of the more than fourteen thousand men who began the attack, fewer than half would return to the safety of their own lines. The ranks of the officers were particularly decimated. Pickett's division suffered most. Nearly two-thirds of his men were cut down, including all three brigade commanders. Every one of the thirteen regimental commanders was killed or wounded.

A Union artillery officer, Lieutenant Henry T. Lee, witnessed Tazewell's fall. During the attack, Lee saw two Confederate officers join hands, jump onto the wall behind which his battery was positioned, and instantly fall.[1] The act so impressed him that when the charge was repulsed, he went to look for Confederates who had been struck down. One, a boy of nineteen, was dead. The other lay dying from a ghastly wound, his jaw shattered. The wounded officer motioned to Lee for a pencil and paper and wrote as follows: "As we approached the wall my cousin and regimental adjutant, Captain (name forgotten) pressed to my side and said: 'It's our turn next, Tazewell.' We grasped hands and jumped on the wall. Send this to my mother so that she may know that her son has lived up to and died according to her ideals."[2]

About six weeks later, Peggy Patton received two letters in one envelope. The earlier letter, dated July 15, had been dictated by Tazewell to a nurse:

My dear Mother

It has now been nearly two weeks since I have been stretched out on this bed of suffering. You will doubtless have heard before this reaches you that I was badly wounded and left in the hands of the enemy. My sufferings and hardships during about two weeks that I was kept out in the field hospital were very great.

I rec'd a wound through the mouth, fracturing the face bone badly on both sides. The doctors seem to agree that the danger of losing my life is small. The wound is serious, annoying and will necessarily be a very long time in getting well.

I can assure you that it was the greatest consolation to me, whilst lying in pain on the dark and cold ground, to look up to that God to whom you so constantly directed my infantile and puerile thoughts, and feel that I was his son by adoption. When friends are far away from you, in sickness and in sorrow, how delightful to be able to contemplate the wonderful salvation unfolded in the bible. Whilst I have been far from being a consistent Christian, I have never let go of my hope in Jesus, and find it inexpressibly dear now. I write these things to show you my spiritual condition, and to ask your prayers continually for me.

I am glad under such adverse circumstances to be able to write so cheerfully. I do not feel that I could do so every day. Sometimes I feel very badly and very weak. I have strong hope however that I shall get well ultimately, and be restored to the fond embraces of my friends in Virginia. To be at the Meadows, at Spring Farm, or in Richmond, with all the family around, would be the highest delight I could experience. I must however put it off for some time. As soon as I am able to travel, I will hurry homeward.

Give my love to all. I write with some difficulty. Should you wish to communicate, address me Col W T Patton, 7thVaInfy, College Hospital near Gettysburg, Pennsylvania. Poor Lewis Williams died a few days after the battle from the effects of a wound. I am very affectionately your son,
—W. T. Patton

The second letter, dated July 24, appeared to be written by the same hand and began with the dreaded words, "It is my sad duty to inform you...." Peggy Patton read that her son Tazewell had died from his wounds at eleven o'clock on the morning of July 21, 1863, six days after his twenty-eighth birthday:

He was aware of the approach of death, and met it as became a soldier and a Christian. He repeated often the words "in Christ alone, perfectly resigned, perfectly resigned." He spoke with great difficulty, but I could understand him repeating the first lines of the Hymn "Rock of ages, cleft for me".... He called for the 14th chapter of Saint John, which was read to him.... From Miss McRea and Miss Sayer of Baltimore, who were his nurses in the hospital... he rec'd the most devoted attention, and much kindness from several Federal officers who were stationed near the hospital.

Shortly after receiving the letter announcing Tazewell's death, Peggy received another note from his nurses, Miss McRea and Miss Sayer. They enclosed a poem cut from a newspaper that they had read to her dying son:

> On the field of battle, Mother, all the night I lay,
> Angels watching o'er me, Mother, 'til the break of day.

The nurses concluded by saying that they would never forget Tazewell's "beautiful chestnut hair on the pillow."[3]

As she folded the note, Peggy Patton broke down in tears for the first time since learning of her son's death. When another of her sons asked her why she was crying, she lifted her head from her hands and defiantly proclaimed, "I am crying because I have only seven sons left to fight the Yankees." Tazewell was cited for gallantry in virtually every battle he fought in. Of the eight Patton brothers, he would be remembered as the most courageous because he had always been the most afraid.[4]

Tazewell's body now lay next to his brother George Smith Patton, who had also been killed in the Civil War at the age of thirty-one. He had been born in Fredericksburg, Virginia, in 1833 and entered VMI at the age of sixteen. Three of his brothers had also attended VMI. George graduated in 1852, second in his class, ranking first in tactics, French, mathematics, Latin, geology, and chemistry.[5] Upon graduation he taught in Richmond for two years, while he studied for the bar in his father's law office. In November 1855 he married Susan Thornton Glassell. The union produced four children. The eldest was born on September 30, 1856, and christened George William Patton. He later changed his middle name to Smith, after his father. The junior George Smith Patton would eventually move to California, marry, and father two children, one of whom was the future World War II general.

The Pattons' military legacy pre-dated the Confederacy. Tazewell and George had a grandfather, Robert Patton, who had fought in the Revolutionary War, as had Hugh Mercer, his father-in-law. Mercer had fled from Scotland on a ship bound for Philadelphia in 1746. A physician in the army of Charles Edward Stuart—"Bonnie Prince Charlie"—he tended to his fellow Scots who had been wounded fighting for their independence.

In the spring of 1755, Mercer took part in a British expedition to Fort Duquesne on the Ohio River. The commander was General Edward Braddock, and the group of officers included George Washington and six other future generals of the American Revolution. When the column was four miles from its target, at what is now Pittsburgh, Pennsylvania, French troops and Indians, who were hiding in the surrounding forest, attacked the army's advance party from three sides. A thousand British troops were killed in the ensuing three-hour battle. Braddock was shot through the lung. Washington miraculously escaped injury when four bullets tore through his coat. Although Hugh Mercer was severely wounded, he would recover and continue to fight in the French and Indian War for another three years.[6]

After the war, Mercer settled in the thriving town of Fredericksburg, Virginia, where he developed friendships and social ties with other Scotch-Irish colonists who shared his anti-government sentiments. Many times the men would gather over rum punch at the Rising Sun tavern. The party included men who would, in the very near future, play important roles in the American Revolution and in the subsequent government of the United States. George Washington was a customer, as was Patrick Henry. Spence Monroe frequented the tavern, sometimes bringing with him his son James, the future president. John Paul Jones and John Marshall, the future chief justice, both drank at the tavern. The proprietor of the Rising Sun was George Weedon, nicknamed "Old Joe Gourd" after the vessel from which he poured his rum punch. He would later serve as a colonel in the Continental Army.

Hugh Mercer married George Weedon's sister-in-law, Isabella Gordon, and they raised five children. Mercer worked as a physician and pharmacist on Caroline Street in Fredericksburg. One of his notable patients was George Washington's mother, Mary. Washington had referred his mother to Mercer because he feared she was developing a drinking problem. When Mercer examined her, he discovered that she was suffering from cancer and had begun to rely on alcohol to ease the pain of the disease. Mercer treated Mary by having her stop by his shop each day, where he administered her a mild opiate.

In the spring of 1775, revolutionary fervor burst into the open with bloody battles at Concord and Lexington. At St. John's Church in Richmond, Virginia, Patrick Henry made his famous declaration, "Give me liberty or give me death!" Other patriotic colonists in Virginia established a committee of safety to protect their rights and buttressed it by forming three regiments of militia. Patrick Henry commanded one, and Hugh Mercer took charge of another. Acceding to command, Mercer patriotically proclaimed, "We are not engaged in a war of ambition or I should not have been here. For my part, I have but one object in view, and that is the success of the cause; and God can witness how cheerfully I would lay down my life to secure it." His words would prove prophetic. Mercer said farewell to his family and departed for Williamsburg. For the second time in his life he was taking up arms against the king of England in the name of freedom.

By the autumn of 1776, the fledgling and underfunded Continental Army seemed near collapse. After defeat and retreat following the battle of Brooklyn, public support as well as recruitment dropped and desertions rose. Even the commander in chief, George Washington, seemed to lose hope. "I think the game is pretty near up," he wrote in an uncharacteristic moment of despair in November. The Continental Army's fortunes, however, were about to change dramatically.

On December 16, General John Armstrong overheard a private discussion between two officers about a secret plan to cross the Delaware and surprise the enemy garrison at Trenton. The two officers were George Washington and Hugh Mercer, who would both participate in the night crossing on Christmas. The attack took the Hessian mercenary defenders completely by surprise. One hundred of the enemy were killed and a thousand captured. The Continentals suffered only four dead. The stunning and inspirational victory provided a huge psychological lift for the army, which might well have disintegrated days later, at the end of the year, when many of the soldiers' enlistments expired.

After the victory at Trenton, Washington set his sights on the British supply depot at nearby Princeton. A spy's map of the area revealed a little-used trail around the British defenses along the Post Road into Princeton. The main body of Washington's troops would follow this trail into town while another four hundred men led by General Mercer proceeded north along Stony Brook to the Post Road bridge. Mercer's objective was the destruction of the bridge in order to block potential British reinforcements from Trenton.

Mercer's men reached the bridge just as British troops were crossing it and leaving town. When Mercer lost the nearby high ground to the British, he decided to rejoin the main column moving toward Princeton. As the men moved across an orchard, they came under attack. The Americans fired a volley at the British, but the more disciplined and better-trained redcoats, who could reload more quickly, returned three volleys before charging Mercer's men with bayonets. Mercer's horse was felled by a musket ball. On foot, he unsuccessfully attempted to rally his men, who soon broke ranks and fled the British assault. Mercer did not flee. He was shot, then bludgeoned about his head with a musket butt. When the enemy discovered his rank, they exulted at taking a "rebel general" and told him to ask for "quarter," that is, to beg that his life be spared. A fearless Mercer refused, and instead defiantly lunged at his nearest tormentor with his sword. He was bayoneted and left for dead.

Washington himself, drawn to the scene by the sound of gunfire, confronted Mercer's fleeing soldiers. "There is but a handful of enemy, and we will have them directly!" he shouted. The scattered men rallied, bolstered by Washington's presence and the sight of a brigade of reinforcements. Washington boldly rode out alone between the revolutionary troops and the approaching British army. He turned his back on the enemy and ordered his troops to prepare to fire. The opposing forces exchanged several volleys before the British fled the field of battle.

The injured Mercer was carried to the home of William Clark, the owner of the orchard in which he had fallen. Clark's wife and daughter tended to his wounds, only to be interrupted by British soldiers who burst into the house and began robbing the helpless general. The delirious Mercer, whose blood had soaked through the straw mattress he lay on, insisted that he had been paroled and was no longer a fugitive from Charles Stuart's rebellion—the revolt in which he had participated thirty-one years earlier in Scotland.

When Washington learned that Mercer was badly wounded but still alive, he sent his nephew George Washington Lewis under a flag of truce to check on Mercer's condition. British General Cornwallis also chivalrously sent his personal surgeon to assist the colonial doctors who were tending Mercer. (Cornwallis may also have been attempting to squelch an uprising of the populace's outrage at the treatment of Mercer as he lay dying on the battlefield.) Arriving at the general's bedside, Lewis lifted Mercer's left arm, revealing a deep puncture wound between the ribs that penetrated to a lung. Mercer knew his wound was mortal. "Yes, sir, that is the fellow that will very soon do my business," he said.

"My death is owing to myself," Mercer told Lewis. He then uttered his own patriotic epitaph: "To die as I had lived, an honored soldier in a just and righteous cause." On January 12, 1777, nine days after the battle, Mercer expired in Lewis's arms. Thirty thousand mourners attended his funeral in Philadelphia. Rumors that Mercer had been bayoneted while attempting to surrender fueled colonial outrage. Two decades later, Jonathan Trumbull would immortalize the fallen revolutionary hero in his painting, *The Death of General Mercer at the Battle of Princeton*. Trumbull's work depicts a defiant Mercer, leaning against his fallen steed, grabbing his assailant's bayonet with one hand and swinging a saber at the enemy with the other. In the background, George Washington rides on horseback to the American's aid.

Fifteen years after Mercer's death, in October 1792, his daughter married a prosperous Virginia businessman named Robert Patton. Like Mercer, Patton was an immigrant from Scotland, but he had declined to serve in the Continental Army. One of Robert Patton's seven children was John Mercer Patton, who himself sired nine sons, among them George Smith Patton. George Patton's eldest, another George (William) Smith Patton, became the father of General George S. Patton, the legendary general of World War II.[7]

CHAPTER TWO

BENJAMIN DAVIS WILSON

"There were no courts, no juries, no lawyers, nor any need for them. The people were honest and hospitable, and their word was as good as their bond..."

—Benjamin Davis Wilson

From his maternal grandfather, Benjamin Davis Wilson, Patton inherited his physical characteristics—height, build, and visage—as well as his temperament. But he had little interest in the Wilson legacy. Patton was descended from two powerful strains of American history. His paternal ancestors were Virginia aristocracy—genteel, well-bred men with professional careers in the law, the ministry, or the military. Benjamin Davis Wilson, on the other hand, represented the rough and egalitarian American West. Both strains were evident in Patton's character, but it was the Virginia pedigree of his father's family to which he was devoted.

Benjamin Davis Wilson, a self-made man who achieved spectacular commercial success, led a life of extraordinary adventure. He was born in Nashville, Tennessee (then the westernmost of the seventeen

United States), on December 1, 1811. Beyond Tennessee lay a continent of wilderness, which President Thomas Jefferson had purchased from France eight years earlier. On the western edge of the continent the Kingdom of Spain clung to its empire. Nestled along the Porciuncula River was the small pueblo of La Reina de los Angeles (Queen of the Angels). Wilson's destiny was entwined with the settlement that became the city of Los Angeles.

Wilson's father died when the boy was only eight years old. At the age of fifteen, Wilson opened a small trading operation on the Yazoo River north of Vicksburg, Mississippi. He quickly moved from trading to fur trapping, selling enough beaver pelts in Santa Fe to fund his own party of trappers. Wilson became one of the thousand or so Rocky Mountain trappers known to American history as the "mountain men." It was a colorful group:

> In his time the mountain man was an Army Ranger, Hell's Angel, Viking and pirate wrapped into one cultural mutant. He left the comforts of the nineteenth century for Stone Age survival in a mostly unmapped, alien landscape of B-movie hazards.... [H]e lived off the land exactly as the Indian had survived in the same environment for thousands of years. He ate what he killed—and he wore what he killed as well—if it didn't kill him first.[1]

Mountain men suffered the predations of Indian tribes, particularly Blackfeet and Comanche, who would steal their horses and their furs. Grizzly bears were another lethal adversary. Most mountain men had at least one encounter with the violent animals and seemed drawn to the thrill of the mortal combat.

During the winter of 1835–1836, Wilson undertook an expedition to the Gila River area. Twenty-three years old and having organized his own small company, he set out with five other trappers. The men went six days without food, and Wilson was forced to shoot his mule to avoid starvation. Worse, they ran out of water, wandering five days before they found a gorge.

On another expedition, Wilson and his party were set upon by an Apache war party seeking revenge for the assassination of their leader, Chief Juan Jose, by an American named James Johnson. Wilson was actually a friend of Jose, though he was unaware of the Indian's murder. Three members of the expedition, including Wilson, were taken prisoner. The Apaches stripped them naked and commenced a war dance, preparing to burn the prisoners alive. Wilson somehow escaped and, over several days, made his way by foot almost two hundred miles to Santa Fe.

By 1841, anti-American sentiment was percolating in New Mexico, a Mexican territory. The region was rife with rumors that Texans, who had gained independence from Mexico five years earlier, planned to foment a liberation movement in New Mexico. Wilson and other foreigners were suspected of complicity in the plot, so he hastily sold his store and made plans to travel to the west coast, intending eventually to make his way to China.

Wilson loaded his possessions onto a pack mule and set out from Santa Fe in a party that eventually numbered 134 people. The diverse group included Jacob Frankfort, soon to be the first Jewish resident of Los Angeles. The travelers drove a flock of sheep, which provided them with food as they made their way west along the Old Spanish Trail to Los Angeles. Their route took them through the southwest corner of Colorado, then north into central and southwest Utah, across the deserts of Nevada to the springs at Las Vegas. Next they crossed the Mojave Desert to the Cajon Pass through the San Bernardino Mountains, finally entering southern California, then still a Mexican territory. They arrived at the San Gabriel mission on November 5, 1841, the first overland settlers' party to travel to the area (most others had arrived by ship or defected from fur-trapping parties).

Wilson had no intention of remaining in another Mexican territory. He traveled three times to San Francisco, each time seeking passage to the Far East, and each time unsuccessful. He eventually abandoned his plans for adventure in China and settled in Alta, California, becoming a ranchero on a large cattle ranch. A year and a half after leaving New Mexico, Wilson purchased for a thousand dollars a ranch of his own—called Rancho Jurupa—in the area that is now Riverside, California. There he found contentment:

> After many unsuccessful efforts to leave California, and receiving so much kindness from the native Californians [Mexicans], I arrived at the conclusion that there was no place in the world where I could enjoy more true happiness and true friendship than among them. There were no courts, no juries, no lawyers, nor any need for them. The people were honest and hospitable, and their word was as good as their bond....[2]

Comfortably settled into the community, Wilson earned enough respect to be asked to serve as *alcalde*, the senior official of the town. The position was comparable to that of mayor, but it combined executive, legislative, and judicial powers. An American citizen, Wilson was technically ineligible under Mexican law to hold such a position, but he accepted at the urging of his friends and to serve his own interests.

A year after acquiring Rancho Jurupa, the thirty-two-year-old "Don Benito," as he was known, put down roots in another way—he married his neighbor's daughter, Ramona Yorba, then only fifteen. Her father, Don Bernardo Yorba, owned 150,000 acres known as Rancho Santa Ana, in what is now Orange County.

Shortly after Wilson's marriage, a large bear killed one of his milk cows. He dutifully went after the bear, tracking it into the woods. When he and his horse became entangled in some wild vines, the bear lunged at them, knocking horse and rider to the ground. The bear tore into Wilson's hip, shoulder, and lung with its teeth before the rancher's dogs scared it off. Ranch hands carried Don Benito home, but he was bleeding so profusely he temporarily lost his sight and speech. The bear continued to ravage the herd while Wilson convalesced. Once he recovered, Wilson pursued the bear again. He had a ranch hand drag a slaughtered calf to the area where the bear had been spotted, and the two men waited in a sycamore tree. At dusk, when the bear showed up, they opened fire. The bear attempted to reach the men in the tree before leaving the scene. The next day Wilson and a new hunting party tracked down the bear at a mud hole where it was nursing its wounds. The indomitable beast once again charged Wilson but was brought down in a hail of gunfire.

In the summer of 1845, Pio Pico, the Mexican governor of California, asked Wilson to lead a campaign against Indian tribes who had harassed ranches in the area. It took three violent forays to pacify the territory. In one fight, Wilson himself was hit in the shoulder by a poisoned arrow.

On June 14, 1846, California's independence was declared in Sonoma. A few weeks later, the United States flag was raised at Monterey. In response to reports that the American military was moving on Los Angeles, Governor Pico asked Wilson to raise troops to repel the foreigners. Wilson uneasily declined, explaining that he was an American citizen and (in spite of his recent raids against the Indians) that he was not a military man. Threatened with arrest, Wilson found himself in a delicate situation. He had no desire to take up arms against the United States, but he had settled happily into the Mexican community, of which he was a respected member. He was fluent in Spanish and had married into a prominent Mexican family. He was the *alcalde* in his district. Wilson pledged that if he was allowed to remain quietly on his ranch, he would "be peaceable, and do no act hostile to the country."[3]

When Commodore Robert Stockton of the U.S. Navy arrived in San Pedro in August, preparing to move against Los Angeles, Mexican forces evacuated the region without a fight. Wilson greeted Stockton when he landed, presented him with a riding horse, and offered to escort him to the center of Los Angeles while providing for his safety. Stockton recognized Wilson's sway in the community and offered him a military command. Wilson gave the same excuse to Stockton that he had given to Pico—he was not a military man. Eventually he was persuaded to accept a commission in the U.S. Army as a captain after securing a guarantee that he would not be required to serve outside of southern California. He was defeated at the Battle of Chino, and Wilson and his men surrendered. Wilson was threatened with execution, but the war ended shortly after his capture, and he was released from prison.

With California part of the United States, Wilson returned to commercial pursuits. He gave up ranching, moved into town, and opened a store in downtown Los Angeles. By 1850 he was one of the four richest men in the county, owning property valued at fifty thousand dollars. After California's admission as a state, Benjamin Davis Wilson was elected the first County Clerk of Los Angeles. In 1851 he was elected mayor of Los Angeles. He subsequently served several terms as a county supervisor and three terms as a state senator.

Ramona died in 1849 after only five years of marriage, leaving two small children. Four years later, Wilson married Margaret Hereford, a young widow. The new marriage produced two daughters, Ruth and Annie. Ruth grew up and married a man from Virginia. On November 11, 1885, in her father's Lake Vineyard house, she gave birth to George S. Patton Jr. Don Benito, who had died eight years earlier, never saw the grandson who would become the celebrated general of World War II. But many of the traits for which that grandson became famous—bravado, courage, a love of adventure, and a fearsome temper—would be recognizable to anyone who knew Benjamin Davis Wilson.

CHAPTER THREE

PAPA

GEORGE (WILLIAM) SMITH PATTON II

*"You have in you good soldier blood—and
the opportunity before you is one to inspire your darndest
effort. Be honorable—brave—clean and you will reap your
merited reward."*

—George (William) Smith Patton II
IN A LETTER TO HIS SON

George William Patton knew something about the horrors of war firsthand. As a young boy, he saw the death and destruction wrought by the Civil War, America's most violent and bloody conflict. The war had claimed his own father, Colonel George Smith Patton, who was wounded by an artillery shell while trying to rally his troops at the battle of Winchester in northern Virginia. The colonel died days later when the wound turned gangrenous and he refused amputation.

After the death of his father, the boy helped to resettle his family in a gutted colonial plantation called Woodberry Forest in Madison County, Virginia. Inside the home they found the decaying corpses of two Yankee soldiers. The boy helped to haul the bodies to an outlying field, where they were buried. Before the bodies were interred, however, George William had to strip them of their clothing. Should the remains ever be found, the family might be accused of murdering Yankees. Naked bodies would presumably never be identified.

Shortly after turning eleven years old, the boy surprised his mother, Susan, by requesting to change his middle name from William to Smith, thus adopting the name of his fallen father. She hesitated. Susan favored her son Glassell, and she doubted that George William could live up to her beloved husband's legacy. When she finally consented, the young boy solemnly said, "I only hope I may be worthy of it." Later on, Glassell severely injured his head in a fall while flying a kite from the roof of a stable, and the legacy of the fallen Colonel Patton became solely George's to uphold.

After the war, Susan Patton moved with her children to southern California to live with her brother. In 1870, she married George Hugh Smith, her first husband's cousin and her brother's law partner. The Patton children came to adore their stepfather. Rather than trying to replace their father's memory, Smith went out of his way to burnish the myth of the children's father with his personal witness to Colonel Patton's wartime exploits and bravery.

Before he was even in his teens, George William had been numbed by the carnage of war and the loss of his father. But wishing to follow the military traditions of his Southern heritage and to honor his father's memory, he enrolled as a cadet at the Virginia Military Institute, which his father had attended. When he returned to Virginia, George reconnected with his grandmother, Peggy Patton. If George was skittish and traumatized from the war, his grandmother was an unreconstructed rebel sympathizer. Shortly before her death, George escorted her in a buggy to Sunday church services. When a dignified former Confederate colonel tipped his hat to Peggy as they passed, she abruptly challenged him, "Tell me, Colonel, did you say 'amen' when the minister prayed for 'the president of the United States and all others in authority'?" Aware that Mrs. Patton had sacrificed two sons in the war against the Union, he nodded cautiously. "Yes, ma'am,

I did. The war is over, after all." Peggy's face tightened, then she seized George's buggy whip and lashed the colonel across his face. "Drive on," she ordered her grandson, handing him back his whip. As a Patton descendant would later note, "Clearly the war wasn't over for her."[1]

After his graduation from VMI, at which he had delivered the valedictory address to the class of 1877, George William decided against a military career and returned to Los Angeles. Southern California had become a popular refuge for former Confederates seeking new lives. The eldest son, he undoubtedly felt compelled to help his struggling family, but perhaps he had also witnessed too much of the death and callousness of war to pursue a profession as a soldier. In the future, he would often wonder if he had let himself down by not pursuing his military ambitions. Had he secretly welcomed the excuse of his family's financial distress to abandon military hardships for a comfortable civilian career? His mixed feelings would haunt him the rest of his life.

George William distinguished himself as a lawyer, becoming the district attorney for Los Angeles and Pasadena. He married Benjamin Davis Wilson's daughter, Ruth. They had two children, George Smith Patton Jr., as he was known—"Georgie" as a child—and Nita. But George William always harbored a secret yearning for the road not taken. He infused his own son with his unfulfilled military ambitions, feeding him the romanticism of war with none of the unvarnished cruelty that he had witnessed as a boy. One summer, though, the father's ambivalent feelings emerged while his son was hunting goats on Catalina Island. In all the years they had hunted and fished together, the father had never carried a gun or dipped a fishing pole into the water. Georgie asked him why. After a long pause, George William quietly answered, "I am a man of peace." It was spoken almost apologetically, as if it were a confession. Yet the father would continue to fuel and assist his son's own military ambitions.

As a confirmation present, Georgie received the leather-bound Book of Common Prayer that his grandfather, Colonel Patton, had carried throughout the Civil War. Georgie's father inscribed it with an invocation of the book's original owner, "who died gloriously at the head of his men, and who in being a soldier did not cease to be also a Christian man." The inscription captured George William's conflicted feelings about the soldier's profession while still nurturing his son's visions of the glory that could be won on the battlefield, even in death.[2]

By the end of the summer of 1902, Georgie had decided on an army career, to the surprise of no one who knew of his years of indoctrination in the Patton heritage. Papa Patton was pleased by his boy's decision, and the two of them decided that Georgie would seek admission to the United States Military Academy at West Point. By attending West Point rather than VMI, Patton would be breaking new ground.

VMI remained an alternative, though, should Georgie not gain admittance to West Point. Given the family legacy, his acceptance at VMI was practically assured. West Point was another matter. Admission was by presidential or congressional appointment after a highly competitive testing of the applicant's scholarship and athletic ability. A victim of undiagnosed dyslexia, Georgie had always struggled academically. But he had one advantage over other competing applicants: the unwavering support and dedicated efforts of Papa Patton.

The elder Patton called upon all the connections he had cultivated over the years in southern California business and politics. Papa decided that the most likely source of an appointment was U.S. Senator Thomas R. Bard, a founder of the UNOCAL oil company, a Union veteran of the Civil War, and a Republican. Bard's next vacancy was in June 1904.

Bard would seem to have been an unlikely benefactor. Patton was a Democrat, and Bard was reputed to have become "a good hater of Rebels." He could hardly have been sympathetic with Georgie's

Confederate pedigree. But the effort to obtain an appointment from Bard would consume Patton for the next eighteen months.

Bard was barraged with letters supporting George Patton's candidacy, each one of which required a response from Bard's personal secretary. The letters came from such notables as John B. Miller, president of the Edison Electric Company; H. E. Huntington, president of the Los Angeles Railway Company; Judge H. T. Lee; and other members of the elite and exclusive California Club. Bard betrayed no sympathy to Patton's candidacy, offering only to give the young man "the opportunity of competing with the other applicants."[3]

Georgie began to doubt that he was good enough to live up to his family's tradition. With his application for an appointment to West Point still pending, Patton prepared to depart for VMI. Just before he left for Virginia, he confessed to a relative his fear that he might be cowardly. He was informed that "no Patton could be a coward."[4] When he shared this exchange with his father, he was told that "while ages of gentility might make a man of my breeding reluctant to engage in a fist fight, the same breeding made him perfectly willing to face death from weapons with a smile."[5]

In September 1903, George Smith Patton Jr. left Lake Vineyard, California, and traveled by train across the continent to Lexington, Virginia, to enroll at the Virginia Military Institute. He was accompanied by his parents, his sister, and his obsessively adoring Aunt Nannie, who remained nearby throughout most of the year. But the question of George's admission to West Point was still unresolved. After his father bade him farewell at VMI, Patton later remembered, "I never felt lower in my life."[6]

Georgie was delighted when the school's long-serving tailor recognized him as a Patton and noted that his uniform measurements were identical to those of his father and grandfather. Patton's academic performance at VMI was a remarkable improvement over his performance in high school. "By February 1904, of the approximately ninety students in his VMI class, Patton stood sixth in drawing, ninth in mathematics, tenth in Latin, and twenty-eighth in both history and English. His deportment was perfect: no demerits, and a well-earned 'Excellent' was handwritten on his report card."[7]

Patton arrived at VMI an ambitious young man who was determined to make good. His father had prepared him extraordinarily well and had provided simple but useful advice—be a good soldier; be a good scholar; and on the nights before you are to march on guard duty, clean and shine your gun and brass until they are spotless. If there was time left over, he was to study. He heeded his father's words, and "the result was that I never walked but one tour of Quarters guard, on all other occasions being [selected as] Orderly."[8]

But Patton remained focused on gaining admission to West Point: "I must get that appointment." Senator Bard, however, was not cooperating. While he might have succumbed to the pressure from Papa Patton and his influential friends among southern California businessmen, lawyers, and judges, Bard instead chose to appoint referees to administer informal competitive examinations. He also telegraphed the VMI superintendent to see if Patton would be released to take the West Point examination in Los Angeles. The superintendent consented, and Georgie returned to California in early February 1904.

It would be the most important date in the young man's life so far. On February 15, George S. Patton's destiny would be decided by how well he did on the competitive examination. The following day he was eastbound for the six-day journey back to VMI. Two and a half weeks later, on March 4, Mr. Patton received a telegram from Senator Bard with the following news: "I have today nominated your son as principal to West Point." The preparation and study had paid off handsomely—Georgie scored first in the competitive examination.

Papa Patton composed a congratulatory letter to his son:

It has been a long and tiresome quest, but in your success I am sure that you will be more than compensated. It is a serious step that you have taken, thus fixing your future career for life and I am sure you have done so with a full appreciation of all that it means.... That which a man desires most strongly to do in this world, if he has really given it careful consideration, is what he is generally most fitted to do.

In a second letter, Mr. Patton wrote: "You cannot know how proud we feel.... You may look forward to an honorable career—as a soldier of your country.... You have in you good soldier blood—and the opportunity before you is one to inspire your darndest effort. Be honorable—brave—clean—and you will reap your merited reward."[9]

Soon after Patton's appointment, Senator Bard was defeated in his bid for reelection. He died in 1915, barely a footnote in history. Perhaps his most momentous act was his appointment of a young man from San Gabriel, California, to West Point: George Smith Patton Jr.

Patton had been at West Point barely a month when he drew the ire of his fellow cadets by unfavorably comparing West Point with VMI. His biographer Carlo D'Este identifies this incident as an early example of Patton's life-long propensity to say the wrong thing in public. "I have been catching a good deal of hell lately because in an unguarded moment I said that we braced [stood at attention] harder at VMI than here. Ever since that accursed speech all the corps have been trying to show me my error and they have succeeded...."[10] He remained firmly set upon fulfilling his life's purpose, however. As he wrote to his father, "Of course I may be a dreamer but I have a firm conviction that I am not and in any case I will do my best to attain what I consider—wrongly perhaps—my destiny."[11]

While at West Point, his ambition and strong sense of purpose were sometimes overwhelmed by despair and self-doubt, which he frequently confessed to his father, as he did in this letter, dated September 4, 1904:

> I don't know whether you knew it or not that I have always thought that I was a military genius or at least that I was or would be a great general. Well looking over the situation as it stands at present I see little in which to base such a belief. I am neither quicker nor brighter in any respect than other men nor do they look upon me as a leader as it is said Napoleon's classmates looked upon him.... I have ideals without strength of character to live up to them.[12]

From a letter to his father dated October 5, 1904: "I am doing rotten.... I am absolutely worthless. I know that I should study and don't. I see my lack of preparation today but tomorrow will be in the same fix."[13]

From a letter to his father dated November 1904: "In fact the sum total of me is that I am a character-less, lazy, stupid yet ambitious dreamer; who will degenerate into a third rate second lieutenant and never command anything more than a platoon."[14]

The young man, in expressing his worst fears, was certainly seeking reassurance and reinforcement more than merely fishing for compliments. With every report of defeat or self-doubt, Patton's father would patiently encourage his son to keep striving to do his best. After his son told him of having tripped over the seventh hurdle in a track race, resulting in a last-place finish, the elder Patton responded with this letter dated June 10, 1905:

> My dear Boy: Your letter of the 3rd came today and I can't tell you how my soul sympathized with you in your defeat in the hurdle race—but it was only because I knew how much you had set your heart on success. It is a good thing

to be ambitious and to strive mightily to win in every contest in which you engage, but you must school yourself to meet defeat and failure without bitterness—and to take your comfort in having striven worthily and done your best.... [T]he real victor is he who strives bravely and *deserves* to win.... So in all life's battles you can find the real heroes among the *apparently* defeated. The honors which are bestowed upon the *apparently* successful ones—are most often the prizes of accident and circumstance....

My dear boy, you do not know how much I miss you—and wish I could be with you and help you bear your disappointments when they come, but I cannot—and indeed would not if I could. You have got to fight your battles alone—to meet victory or defeat as becomes a man and a gentleman....

I have no fears for you—I know you are doing your best—and that is all you can do. When you have done that—for me you have *won*.[15]

George's difficult first year at West Point ended with a major setback. He failed mathematics and would have to repeat his plebe year. After a summer at Lake Vineyard and Catalina, he prepared to depart for West Point again. Before he left, he purchased a small notebook in which he could keep a record of events and scribble down his thoughts. His first entry: "Do your damdest always."

There were other telling entries in Patton's journal:

* By perseverance and study and eternal desire any man can be great.
* If you die not a soldier and having had a chance to be one I pray God to damn you George Patton.

* ⋆ Never never never stop being ambitious… you have but one life live it to the full glory and be willing to pay.
* ⋆ Nothing is too small to do to win.
* ⋆ If you infringe your honor you have sold your soul.
* ⋆ We live in deeds not years.
* ⋆ You can be what you will to be.
* ⋆ You have done your damndest and failed now you must do your damndest and win.

Patton's West Point years were somewhat solitary. As his biographer Martin Blumenson notes,

> His classmates regarded George Patton with some ambivalent emotions. They accepted him generally with affection and admiration for his sincerity, candor, and fairness. They smiled in condescension over his naïve earnestness and enthusiasm. They believed that he tried too hard, had too much spirit, and they were uncomfortable with his obsessive concern with future glory, which he could not resist confessing from time to time.
>
> He had no close friends.[16]

Patton's nicknames at West Point were "Georgie" and "Quill"—in West Point slang, to "quill" meant to report someone for an offense. Patton was considered a "quilloid," one who demanded an impossible sort of perfection and who would not hesitate to report those who failed to live up to the strictest interpretation of the rules. The class Furlough Book noted that Patton "stands erect, right martial in his air, his form and movements." He was also judged to be a "bootlick," one who curried favors with his superiors, not exactly a compliment. The 1909 *Howitzer*, the West Point yearbook, noted, "We believe that Georgie's heart, despite its armored exterior, has a big soft spot inside…."

During his senior year, Patton turned again to his father for help with another momentous decision, one in which his worst fears and insecurities ambushed his ambitions. He would later write, "The winter before I graduated Papa was at West Point and I had a long talk with him in the library. I said that I was in love with Beatrice but was afraid to propose. Papa encouraged me to do so, I did, only to be accepted."[17] Patton's father had thus assisted in securing the two biggest anchors of his son's future, his admission to West Point, with his subsequent success there; and his engagement to the woman who would in many ways become the new prop in Patton's life, buttressing him against his career's many setbacks.

In the spring of 1926, Patton's parents and his sister, Nita, visited Hawaii, where he was now stationed. The warm family union made it a happy time, with extensive doting on the recently born George Patton, the new heir and bearer of the family name. The only black cloud at the gathering was the obviously serious decline in the health of the family's patriarch. Facing his mortality, the elder Patton expressed his wish that the family all come home to California for "one more Christmas together." The Pattons dutifully returned to the Lake Vineyard home for the Christmas holidays. The dying Papa assured George that history was saving a special place for him, that his military career was a matter of fate, and that he was being prepared to fulfill some special role. He confidently predicted that George would serve in the greatest war in history. The son needed little assuring. He had always believed the same about himself.

Two months later, his father's condition worsened, and in February 1927 a life-saving operation was attempted. Patton, who had just returned to Hawaii, rushed back to California in time to kiss his father as he was being wheeled into surgery. Watching the old man, evidently in great pain, the son wondered if his father would survive the trauma of surgery. He was struck by his father's courage—how, facing what he thought was death, the father sought to bolster his son's spirit without thinking of himself. The father survived, and while he recovered the son waited by his side for three weeks before returning to duty in Hawaii. The night before he left, he kissed his father for what would be the last time and said good-bye. The father smiled weakly and uttered his final words to his son: "Good-bye, Old Man. Take care of yourself."[18]

In June 1927 the dreaded telegram arrived in Hawaii announcing Papa's passing. The cause of death was probably a latent case of tuberculosis, thought to have been contracted from his uncle, William Glassell, a Confederate naval officer, who had acquired it in a Civil War POW camp. Years of excessive drinking, resulting in cirrhosis of the liver, also certainly contributed to his death.

There was no ship leaving Hawaii for California at that time, and Patton missed his father's funeral. He was inconsolable, blaming himself for not having been at his father's side when he died, "for not having been there when Bamps needed him, and for having spent so much of his life away from home; for all the little things he might have done for his father." Beatrice, his wife, was also devastated by the loss of a man she had known her entire life. She considered Papa Patton more as a second father than a father-in-law. She tried unsuccessfully to comfort her despairing husband by reminding him that he had always been a dutiful son.[19]

Patton made his three children memorize the poem "After Death in Arabia" by Sir Edwin Arnold, in which the deceased chides his friends for mourning his passing, pointing out that his soul still lives on, having merely cast away its mortal frame:

> Faithful friends! It lies, I know,
> Pale and white and cold as snow;
> And ye say, "Abdallah's dead!"
> Weeping at the feet and head.
> I can see your falling tears,

I can hear your sighs and prayers;
Yet I smile and whisper this,—
"*I* am not the thing you kiss;
Cease your tears, and let it lie;
It *was* mine, it is not I."
Sweet friends! What the women lave
For its last bed of the grave,
Is a tent which I am quitting,
Is a garment no more fitting,
Like a hawk my soul hath pass'd.
Love the inmate, not the room—
The wearer, not the garb,—the plume
Of the falcon, not the bars
Which kept him from these splendid stars.

Patton's daughter, Ruth Ellen, later wrote that the poem "has seen us through everything that has ever happened to us in the grief of our later years."[20]

Carlo D'Este writes that his father's death "was the most traumatic event of Patton's life. He had lost the best friend he ever had, and the man who had sacrificed so much for a son he adored."[21] Patton poured his emotions into a touching memoir of his father in which he reveals the depth of his feelings toward the man who had nurtured his ambitions from boyhood:

> The morning I arrived I wore my uniform and went alone to his grave. The whole lot was covered with flowers all which had wilted save the pall of red roses over the spot where he lay. These to me seemed fresh, vivified by the great soul of him who lay beneath them.
>
> For an hour I stood there and the knowledge came to me that the grave no more held Papa than does one of his

discarded suits hanging in a closet. Suddenly I seemed to see him in the road wearing his checked overcoat and with his stick which he waved at me as he had been used to do when I was impatient and wanted to go somewhere.

I knelt and kissed the ground then put on my cap and saluted not Papa, but the last resting place of that beautiful body I had loved. His soul was with me and but for the density of my fleshly eyes I could have seen and talked with him.

A few days later, Patton had a second vision of his deceased Papa. Seated at his father's desk, poring over the contents of his safe, Patton handled the minie ball that had killed his great uncle Waller Tazewell at Gettysburg and the shell fragment that had killed his grandfather at Winchester. Tears began streaming down his face as Patton looked up to see his father standing in the doorway. He was frowning and seemed to be shaking his head. To Patton, the message was that everything was well and that his father was admonishing him not to mourn for him. Once Patton mentally acknowledged this message, his father smiled radiantly, turned, and walked to the stairs. Only when his father disappeared did Patton remember that the man had been dead and in his grave for five days.[22]

As I write this in his office where we talked and smoked so often he is here. I like to remember not the symbol of his gallant spirit which I saluted in the church yard but rather Papa as he was wheeled out to die perhaps, and to think of his words so true of our present temporary separation when he smiled at me and said "Au revoir Son."

Oh! Darling Papa. I never called you that in life as both of us were too self contained but you were and are my darling. I have often thought that life for me was too easy but the loss of you has gone far [to] even my count with those whom before I have pitied.

God grant that you see and appreciate my very piteous attempt to show here your lovely life. I never did much for you and you did all for me. Accept this as a slight offering of what I would have done.

Your devoted son

—*G S Patton Jr*

July 9 1927[23]

CHAPTER FOUR

DEAREST BEA

BEATRICE AYER PATTON

"May our love never be less than now and our ambition as fortunate and as great as our love."

—Patton's letter to his fiancée
Beatrice Ayer before their wedding

Beatrice Ayer rejected her first opportunity to meet her future husband, George Patton, in 1892. She was six years old, and her family had traveled from their home in Boston to visit the Bannings, wealthy relatives in Wilmington, California, twenty miles south of Los Angeles. The Ayer family planned a day trip to Los Angeles to see other relatives. The strong-minded Beatrice refused to participate in the excursion. Carriage rides made her slightly sick, and she had a new book that she wanted to read, so she stayed behind at the Banning mansion. When the family returned, they spoke about their wonderful visit with their cousins, including young Hancock Banning's new wife, the former Miss Smith. The bride's father, Colonel Smith, had been there with his stepson's family, the Pattons. One of them was a dear little boy, they told Bea, whose name was "Georgie."

He was just a few months older than Beatrice and had beautiful, big blue eyes and lovely golden curls. He was such a good little boy, Bea's mother admonished gently, that he would never have let his father and mother and brother go off alone just so he could read a book. Resenting her mother's subtle reproof, Beatrice decided then and there that Georgie Patton must be a little prig. She retorted that she hoped never to meet him, and if she did, she would certainly not play with him.

The next encounter came ten years later and was equally ill-fated. Returning to California in the summer of 1902, the Ayers were met at the train station by a veritable reception committee of relatives. Among them was sixteen-year-old George Patton, preparing to enter VMI in the fall. The Ayers hoped he would introduce Bea to his friends, providing her with an instant social circle so she could fully enjoy the summer. The girl's long braided auburn hair fell to the hem of her skirt, and though she had already received three proposals of marriage, she still carried her beloved doll, Marguerite, under her arm. When he laid eyes on Beatrice, George recoiled, disgusted by what he saw. In Los Angeles in those days, fashionable young ladies wore their hair up, and they most certainly did not play with dolls. He had no intention of inviting the mockery of his friends by escorting this child around.

Patton's views regarding young Beatrice dramatically evolved over the course of that summer. The families' youngsters staged the romantic fantasy *Undine*, by the German novelist Friedrich de la Motte Fouqué. The story is similar to *The Little Mermaid* and was one of the most popular fairy tales of the nineteenth century. Beatrice had the leading role, Undine, the water spirit, with George in the supporting role of Kuhlborn. Their daughter Ruth records in her memoir, *The Button Box*, "By the end of the rehearsals, the play and the summer, Ma and Georgie were in love—as they would be for the rest of their lives."[1]

Theatricals came naturally to Beatrice Ayer, whose mother, Ellen Banning ("Ellie"), was an amateur actress. The intensity of Ellie's devotion to the theater is apparent in her account to Beatrice of how she met her husband. Ellie had accepted an invitation to a party where she was to meet "a great catch"—an older man, a wealthy widower named Frederick Ayer. On the day of the party, Ellie discovered that the legendary Edwin Booth—the greatest Hamlet of his day and the brother of Lincoln's assassin, John Wilkes Booth—was performing his signature role that very evening. Ellie sent a note of apology, explaining her reason for missing the party, then went off to watch the play. As she left the theater, Ellie was approached by "the handsomest man… I had ever seen." The stranger asked if she was Miss Ellen Banning. Social protocol forbade women to be "picked up" by strange men on the street, so Ellie acknowledged who she was and quickly began to move away. But as she would confess to her daughter, "Once I looked into those piercing blue eyes, if he had said 'Ellen Banning, will you follow me to the world's end?' I would have gone right with him just as I was."

The gentleman, of course, was Frederick Ayer. Walking beside her, he smoothly explained, "Miss Banning, when I understood that there was one young lady in the town of such good sense and judgment that she preferred going to see a performance by America's greatest living actor to going to an evening party, I decided that she should have both treats, and I have come for you in my carriage with a chaperone to take you to the party." To Ellie, Frederick Ayer was like a knight in shining armor, and from then on her name for him was always Sir Frederick.

Frederick Ayer's long life (1822–1918) was a perfect specimen of the American dream. He worked at a store as a youngster, sleeping under the counter at night. He owned the store before he was thirty-five. In 1855, he started a patent medicine business with his older brother, Dr. James Cook Ayer. Frederick later moved into the textile business and built a fortune in the mills of Lowell and Lawrence, Massachusetts.

During the Civil War, Ayer and some business associates visited Washington, D.C., and stopped at the White House to meet the president, as was customary then. Ayer found Abraham Lincoln "hard at work in his office, tireless, vest unbuttoned, and in his shirt sleeves, wet with perspiration." He recalled that "Mr. Lincoln received us standing, and looked terribly tired, bored and lifeless until, after introducing myself and our friends, I said, 'Mr. President, I have called to pay our respects to our President, but none of us has a favor to ask, not even a country post office.' At this, he woke up and rushed at me with both hands, took both of mine, and shaking them vigorously said, 'Gentlemen, I am glad to see you. You are the first men that I have seen since I have been here that didn't want something.'"

Ayer was thirty years older than Ellie. His first wife, Cornelia, had died shortly after the birth of their fourth child. Frederick and Ellie had three children together—Beatrice, Frederick Jr., and Mary Katherine, known as Kay. Their granddaughter Ruth Ellen remembered that "[t]he Pattons, who were very different from the Ayers, had several stories they told about Ellie—I don't think they ever knew quite what to make of her." One evening at a large family dinner, Ellie made her entrance, late of course, after everyone else had been seated. Wrapped in lace shawls and with a red rose in her pretty curls, she stood in the dining room door long enough to attract everyone's attention and then seated herself at the right of Mr. Patton, her son-in-law's father. When the conversation turned to politics, and away from Ellie, she took a calculating look around the table, rose, and approached the person seated farthest from her, who happened to be Annie Banning. All conversation stopped. She took Annie's chin in her hand, cluttered with rings, and asked dramatically, "Annie, dear, *what do you think of life?*" The moment made an indelible impression on the Pattons. Someone could always break the tension in family relations by suddenly demanding, "What do you think of life?"

In 1896, Frederick Ayer's doctors recommended that he retire from business. The strong-minded Ayer protested that, as he was only seventy-three years old, he was still in the prime of his working years. He finally relented when his wife tactfully suggested that a sojourn in Europe would give their children the opportunity to learn French. So, with an entourage of governesses and a tutor, the family went abroad for two years.

The Ayers spent one memorable winter on a mule-drawn house-boat on the Nile. When Beatrice's half-brother Jamie, a doctor, removed a palm thorn from the foot of an Egyptian laborer, the word spread quickly that there was a physician on board the boat. After that, wherever the houseboat moored for the night, the infirm, the lame, and the blind would crowd about seeking medical attention. Lacking proper medical equipment, Jamie tended to them as best he could.

Naturally curious, Beatrice was thrilled when their boatman's thirteen-year-old son, who served as interpreter, brought her and her brother Freddie to a newly excavated tomb. Beatrice rushed up and was about to jump in, "in case she might find something." The young guide grabbed her just before she leapt into a pit of cobras. She recalled that the snakes, startled by the youngsters' presence, came out of the shadowy recesses of the ancient structure, hissing and spreading their hoods. Beatrice was able to enter another tomb, where a partially unwrapped, 4,000-year-old mummy lay outside of its case. On an impulse, Beatrice broke off a toe from the mummy and took it with her. She kept the relic in a jelly jar the rest of her life.

Young Beatrice also came to admire the tattoo on the back of the boatman who steered the barge. With the guidance of his son, and with a ten-dollar birthday gift from her half-brother, she was led off to the tattoo parlor where the boatman had received the artwork that

Beatrice so admired. The future debutante was intent on having a full-rigged ship inked across her chest, abetted by the encouragement of her young Egyptian friend. Her governess discovered her just in time to prevent a permanent memento of her Egyptian adventure from being etched onto her young body.

When the Ayers returned to America, they moved from industrial Lowell to 395 Commonwealth Avenue in Boston, a stunning townhouse in the upscale Back Bay designed by Louis Comfort Tiffany. The home was full of Tiffany glass, parquet floors, marble inlay, and velvet and lace curtains, and it was a showcase of modern technology—bathrooms, an elevator, a telephone, electricity, and a dumbwaiter. But it was also considered brash by the "old money" of Boston, who were more likely to fill their own residences with jade collections and Georgian antiques.

George Patton's transfer from VMI to West Point gave him the opportunity to spend more time with the Ayers in nearby Boston. He conveyed his already serious attachment to Beatrice in a letter to his mother:

> The Ayers are so awfully nice that it is positively oppressive. We ride, swim, sail, motor and see Bee. Be sure though, I have not told her that she is the only girl I have ever loved, but she is—though it would be fatal for me to mention that fact now or perhaps ever. She is very nice to me and I think likes me for she has been wearing my favorite color dresses ever since I said I liked them. Gosh, those skirted bipeds at Catalina, who pawn themselves off as girls, aren't in it with her shadow. But, O Lord, what an ass I am!

The otherwise self-confident Patton was always curiously insecure about his wife's devotion. As their daughter Ruth noted, "It never occurred to Georgie that Ma was in love with him—he was too humble at that point in his life—and his failure to pass [his first year at West Point] had humbled him even more deeply, but I am sure his parents knew she loved him, as did hers." In a notebook that he kept at West Point, he wrote in January 1909, "Should a man get married he must be just as careful to keep his wife's love as he was to get it. That is he should always be spoony and make love to her so she will continue to like him for it would make her most sad if he said as it were 'Now I have got you I will take a rest.' Don't do that ever."[2]

The couple's courtship during Patton's West Point years consisted of football games and Saturday night dances, picnics and the constant exchange of letters. He spent most of his short leaves with the Ayers, and Beatrice would occasionally travel to California during the summers to spend time with the Pattons and her relatives the Bannings. While Beatrice was recovering from an appendectomy, her siblings, Freddie and Kay, wrote a song to poke fun at her romance with Patton:

> Georgie, Porgie, so they say
> Goes a-courting every day
> Sword and pistol by his side
> Beatrice Ayer for his bride
> Doctor, Doctor, can you tell
> What will make poor Beatrice well?
> She is sick and she might die
> That would make poor Georgie cry.
> Down in the valley where the green grass grows
> There sits Beatrice, sweet as a rose
> And she sings and she sings, and she sings all day
> And she sings for Georgie to pass that way.

After six years of courtship, George Patton finally proposed to Beatrice Ayer in December 1909. He was spending the Christmas

furlough of his senior year with the Ayer family in Boston. Patton was
so afraid that she would refuse him that he carried in his pocket a
phony telegram ordering him back to West Point; if she refused his
proposal, he could produce the telegram and make a hasty retreat.
The nervous cadet postponed the conversation as long as possible. On
a Wednesday afternoon, when the couple found themselves alone in
the library of the Ayers' home, he expressed his love for Beatrice and
his interest in marrying her. Beatrice reciprocated his love, but Patton
insisted that she not accept his proposal until his return from an
expected deployment to the Philippines. He was chivalrously determined, as he would relate in a letter to his mother, that "I alone (as I
have ever been) be bound."

The one obstacle to the marriage was raised by Beatrice's father.
Frederick Ayer was fond of Patton but disapproved of the young man's
choice of career. A life of dusty and dilapidated military housing in
far-flung outposts was not what the protective father had in mind for
his precious daughter. Responding to Patton's request to speak to him,
Ayer wrote:

> My dear George,
>
> Your letter of the 18th is very clear and comprehensive.
> Your ambition I admire. Your "plan of life" is alright if you
> can have a command for a year in God's country and not in
> the Philippines.
>
> Fighting malaria is not war. After all, as the civil life is
> what you finally fall back upon for an indefinite period, the
> question may occur to you whether this first year will not
> be worth more to you in that than in any command you can
> get. That is a question no one can decide for you. You too
> can best judge how much opportunity a year's command
> will give you to investigate and decide upon another occu-
> pation. Always keeping in mind that the younger a man

starts in business the easier it is for him and the better his chance for success.

In regard to speaking to Beatrice, there are times in one's life when one feels impelled to speak and to follow that impulse, which comes after long thought, is natural and generally wise.

Hoping you will pardon the above suggestions, I am
Sincerely yours
—*F. Ayer*

Ayer wrote again, elaborating on his objections to Patton's military career:

Referring to your profession, I believe it is narrowing in its tendency. A man in the army must develop mainly in one direction, always feel unsettled, and that his location and homelife are, in a measure, subject to the dictation and possible freak of another who he may despise or even hate.

This is no reflection on your educational institution which I suppose to be one of the best.

It appears to me that a man like you should be independent of such control. His own man, free to act and develop in the open world.

I would compare the military man to a tree grown in the forest as against one in the field with plenty of room to spread. Should you, at any time, adopt civil life, I have no doubt that your skill and patriotism will be in requisition with equal chance of preferment, as if you had remained in the service.

The exchange of letters continued, with Ayer appealing to Patton's pride in his military training while trying to steer him to a career in commerce, in which that training would be put to good use. Ayer's palpable distaste for the hardships of military life was shared by many New Englanders, to whom the military heritage of Patton's Virginia forebears was quite alien.

The two stubborn men reached a stalemate. Ayer appealed to George's love for Beatrice—if he truly loved her he would do the decent thing: resign his commission and take a job in Boston. Patton responded strategically and emotionally—if he could not marry Beatrice then he would marry no one, but the army had been his passion from early boyhood, and he would not be diverted from his chosen career. Beatrice proved just as stubborn. She locked herself in her bedroom and went on a hunger strike. (Although her younger sister Kay sustained her with a midnight delivery of food in a basket dangled by a string down the stairwell.) Not surprisingly, Beatrice, the daughter of the amateur actress Ellie Banning, delivered an effective, dramatic performance. After a week, Frederick Ayer bowed to the inevitability of the union and gave his assent. In his letter of capitulation to Patton, Ayer acknowledged the young man's military vocation. Henceforth, he wrote, each would do what he did best—Ayer would earn the money, and George would earn the glory.

For her engagement ring, Beatrice eschewed the traditional diamond and accepted a miniature of her fiancé's 1909 West Point class ring, set with a topaz, her future husband's birthstone.

Four days before their wedding, Patton wrote Beatrice a final letter, which displayed eloquence, romance, and ambition:

> Darling Beatrice:
>   This is the last letter I shall write you as your lover only hereafter I shall still be your lover but also your husband. Darling since I wrote my first letter to you almost eight years ago I have grown older and wiser and have thus been

enabled to better understand and more clearly see your infinite perfection. So that in a way I may be said to love you more now than then... for I have ever loved you to the fullest of my power. God grant that if I develop in no other way my capacity for loving you may increase for it is only by a divine love that I can express to you my gratitude for all you are, have been, and will be to me....

I can hardly comprehend that we are hence forth to be one....

I have prayed that you should love and marry me yet not at the expense of your happiness so now that my prayer is to be granted it seems certain that you will be happy. God grant it! May our love never be less than now and our ambition as fortunate and as great as our love. Amen.

—*George*[3]

The couple's wedding took place on May 26, 1910, and was the social event of the year on the fashionable North Shore of Massachusetts. Beatrice wore the wedding dress that had been made for her mother in 1884. The gown was trimmed with orange blossoms shipped from the Pattons' family estate at Lake Vineyard. The groom and the ushers, except for Freddie Ayer, wore their full dress blue uniforms.

Beatrice and George spent their wedding night in a Boston hotel before departing for their honeymoon in Europe. The morning after the wedding, they arranged for room service, but when the knock came at the door, their breakfast was preceded by Ellie, carrying a single white rose in a crystal vase. She was followed by several family members, all of whom had been corralled into rising early for the long train ride to Boston to be there when "the children" awoke. Beatrice thought it a touching gesture, but the more proper, and shy, George Patton almost died of embarrassment.

The honeymoon in England was Patton's first visit to a foreign country. The newlyweds landed in Plymouth on June 3 and spent several days exploring Cornwall. Patton purchased a copy of Clause-witz's classic, *On War*, one of the first volumes in what became his immense military library.[4]

Four months after their wedding, Beatrice announced that she was pregnant. For the new Mrs. Patton, bearing a child for her husband was the culmination of a woman's life. She had been raised in a large, close-knit family, and she looked forward to the addition of a child with natural joy. George seemed to feel more than a twinge of jealousy at the idea of sharing the attention of his new bride. He had been raised as the golden child, the adored center of attention. Now he was threatened with being displaced and seemed slightly resentful at the prospect of a new Patton.

Beatrice, undoubtedly feeling pressure to perpetuate the proud Patton name, approached her husband with a delicate question: "Will you mind terribly if this one is a girl?" Patton answered with what his wife considered the perfect answer: "What do *you* think Beaty? I married one, didn't I?"

And so on March 19, 1911, just at sunset, as the army band at Fort Sheridan was playing the last bars of "The Star-Spangled Banner," Beatrice Ayer Patton was born in Quarters 92A. Patton's wife had wanted to share the moment with her husband and had insisted that he be present for what turned out to be a difficult childbirth. Crowding the little bedroom were the mother, the doctor, a nurse whom the Ayers had brought with them from Boston, and George. The Ayers stayed outside on the landing. George, who had seen plenty of animals birthed growing up, found the sight of his wife suffering in childbirth to be awful and revolting. He never got over it. When the baby was brought over to him, he rushed out of the room and into the kitchen where he vomited into the sink.

Some time later, still adjusting to life as an army wife and to her new responsibilities as a mother, Beatrice received an unexpected call at noon from the base commander's wife, Mrs. Gerard. After inquiring politely about the Patton and Ayer families and about little Bee, the newborn, she asked Beatrice, with considerable discomfort, if the baby had made any difference in their marital happiness. Were she and Mr. Patton getting along happily "in the bedroom"? Beatrice was of course embarrassed and offended, so the equally uncomfortable Mrs. Gerard confessed, "I know you must think me an interfering old woman, Mrs. Patton, but when Colonel Gerard came home at noon for his lunch, he mentioned the fact that Mr. Patton [who was instructing the new recruits in shooting] had been standing on the rifle butts all morning, between the targets, and he wondered if some circumstances had occurred of such a nature that Mr. Patton was trying to take his own life without causing any comment, perhaps because of some misunderstanding at home. As you know, the recruits were firing this morning and they are very green."

Beatrice quickly managed to set Mrs. Gerard's mind at ease about the couple's marital happiness, but when George returned that evening, he was astounded to find his infuriated wife all packed up, ready to take a taxi with her maid and baby to Chicago, to catch a train to Boston. Patton tried to explain that he was only trying to find out what George Washington had meant when he wrote to "his dearest Patsy" that he had heard the bullets whistling past his ears and that "indeed, there was something very merry in the sound." Patton was forever testing his courage, and he confessed that he had also wanted to see if he would be scared while being shot at. His wife was eventually persuaded not to leave, but she remained less than satisfied with her husband's rashness.

Early in his career, Patton was detailed to the École Militaire in Saumur, France. Beatrice reveled in returning to France, speaking the language, sightseeing, and enjoying the food and culture. Patton, already an expert fencer, studied under a renowned swordsman at the Saumur academy while roaming ancient battlefields.

As the family prepared to return to America, Beatrice was left to pack their belongings while George attended the fencing academy. The day before they departed, Patton casually remarked to his exhausted wife, "I hope you remembered to pack all those swords under the bed." Walking into the bedroom, Beatrice discovered dozens of swords and scabbards of which she had been completely unaware. Frustrated that her husband had not appreciated her efforts or informed her of the swords he had been collecting, she angrily picked up one of the weapons and began chasing him around the house. A frantic Patton scurried over chairs and tables, pleading with his furious wife, "Don't! Don't! Please don't!" Beatrice eventually brought the sword down on a table, missing her husband, but hard enough to embed the sword in the edge of the table. A newly compliant husband now offered to help his wife pack his collection.

A second child was born to the Pattons on February 28, 1915, at the Lake Vineyard estate of George's parents, near present-day San Gabriel, just east of downtown Los Angeles. They named her Ruth Ellen, after her grandmothers. Patton himself was away at Fort Riley, Kansas, but he wrote to his father in advance of the birth, "Tell the doctor if there is any question between her life and the life of the child, the child must go." If the doctor would not agree, he wrote, they must find another doctor.

The arrival of another girl produced palpable disappointment in the Patton household. That evening, when Beatrice was propped up on pillows and receiving congratulatory telegrams and flowers, her mother-in-law, whom she called Aunt Ruth, came in to check on her. Feeling that she had failed her in-laws again by producing another girl, Beatrice said, "Well, Aunt Ruth, better luck next time!" The elder Mrs. Patton turned to her with a horrified look and said, "Beatrice dear, please don't mention 'next time' to your Uncle George. He has had a very hard day!"

Frederick Ayer died of pneumonia in March 1918 at the age of ninety-five. Ellie died three weeks later. It was a double tragedy for Beatrice Patton. She had known her father's advanced age made death a constant companion, but she had no idea that her mother was in such poor health. The doctor told Beatrice that her mother must have died "of a broken heart."

Patton was in France when his father-in-law died, training the Tank Corps during World War I. Had the war not broken out in Europe, the Pattons almost certainly would have been stationed in the Philippines. Since wives were forbidden to join their husbands fighting in Europe, Beatrice was able to be with her father when he died. In one of his most compassionate letters, Patton wrote to his wife:

> [I]t is without question a direct interposition of Almighty God that this war made it necessary and possible for you to be with him for had it not occurred you would have been in the Philippines and absent at the time so priceless to him.[5]
>
> Beatrice Jr. and Ruth Ellen should be wonderful children with such a grandfather. It is futile to attempt to comfort you. Words, especially written words, are totally inadequate to console for such a loss.... I know Darling that you are suffering all that the human soul can suffer.... Beaty my whole heart is at your feet.... My poor Darling please take comfort if you can. May God help and strengthen you.[6]

In a second letter to Beatrice after Ellie's death, Patton wrote:

> It seems a heartless thing to say but I think that Ellie is happier than she would have been to have continued on without your father. They were nearly as one as is possible to be—as nearly as one as we are. I do not think I would care much about keeping on if you were gone. Because if you were not around to admire what I did what the rest thought would make little difference.[7]

Beatrice was musically talented. In middle age, she gathered the songs she had written into a little book, which she privately published for family and close friends. One of the songs, titled "Absent," was dedicated to her mother.

> I feel I am not all bereft of her so dear
> For when she went away she left her laughter here,
> A spirit in this room it dwells, and every night
> When I sit here alone, it tells of her delight.
> Her joy in life, it was so wild, that all her days
> She never ceased to be a child, with her wild ways,
> A child, and yet a woman too, could laugh, could weep—
> Her heart was pure, her friendship true, her passion deep.
> Her gentle laughter, soft and low, is in the air.
> None else can hear it, but I know it is there.

Patton was stationed at Fort Myer, across the Potomac from Washington, D.C., four times, beginning in the 1920s. It was in the capital that Beatrice demonstrated how fiercely protective of her husband she could be. One evening while waiting for Patton to park their car at a dinner party, she found herself standing in a foyer next to an older officer. When Patton appeared still wearing his wartime brevet insignia of colonel, the officer remarked dismissively, "Just look at the little boys they are promoting to colonel these days; look at the young chicken still wet behind the ears, wearing a colonel's eagle." The next thing Beatrice remembered was sitting astride the old officer's shoulders, bouncing his head against the black and white marble tiles until her astonished husband and several dinner guests pulled her off the tactless old man.

In 1922, a blizzard dropped twenty-eight inches of snow on Washington. The flat roof of the Knickerbocker movie theater collapsed under the weight, killing ninety-eight people and injuring another hundred. Troops from Fort Myer, including Patton, were dispatched to the scene. He returned home late at night, exhausted, filthy, and traumatized, and recounted for his wife and children the horrors he had seen. "He told us that he and a soldier were trying to free a lady from a collapsed wall and, as they pulled her body out by the legs, her head came off." When his wife objected that the little girls were too young to hear such gruesome stories, George protested, "Bee, goddamit, they've got to know things like that do happen. They can't go through life with blinders on."

Patton worried about getting old. He worried about his hair loss, which continued despite his use of his father-in-law's hair tonic. He worried about developing a middle-aged paunch and for years would continually try on his cadet uniform to see if he could still fit into it. On his fiftieth birthday, he stubbornly refused to get out of bed, feeling that he had missed his chance to make his way into the history books. Other conquering heroes had realized their destiny before fifty. His daughter Ruth Ellen writes, "Caesar had conquered Gaul when he was in his thirties and forties; Alexander had conquered the known world in his thirties; Napoleon was finished at fifty. Ma finally got him out of bed by persuading him that he had been fifty for a whole year without knowing it."

Beatrice, however, aged gracefully and unselfconsciously. "I only remember once," writes Ruth Ellen, "when she was in her late forties,

I found her weeping bitterly in front of her dressing table mirror. When I asked her what was wrong, she wailed, 'Oh, no one that ever sees me now would ever know what a pretty girl I was!' Ma aged naturally. She didn't wear any makeup, and she refused to tint her hair because she had a great, if concealed, contempt for women whom she referred to as 'mutton dressed as lamb.' But to know her was to love her, and she was certainly of 'infinite variety.'"

Beatrice bought her husband a book titled *Change of Life in Men*, hoping it would help him adjust to middle age. The gift infuriated him, and he promptly burned it in the alley behind his house. Without a war on, and fearing his destiny had slipped away, Patton became more difficult to live with. Peace was hell on George Patton. He drank more, and his wife, who had almost never criticized him, spoke to him about it. This intervention had the unintended effect of provoking Patton, and he would sometimes take another drink while his wife was watching as if to make the point. He sought the company of younger people and was open to the flattery of other women.

One of those women, Jean Gordon, apparently succeeded in getting more than George Patton's attention. Jean was an "unusually attractive girl," a first cousin and best friend of Patton's daughter Ruth Ellen. She visited while the Pattons were stationed in Hawaii, just before the outbreak of World War II, when George seemed most distraught that his life's purpose had evaded him. When Jean left Hawaii, Beatrice said to Ruth Ellen, "You know, it's lucky for us that I don't have a mother because, if I did, I'd pack up and go home to her now, and your father needs me. He doesn't know it right now, but he needs me. In fact, right now he needs me more than I need him." She looked away for a moment and then with tears in her eyes continued, "Perhaps there is a reason for all of this. I want you to remember this; that even the best and truest of men can be bedazzled and make fools of themselves. So, if your husband ever does this to you, you can remember that I didn't leave your father. I stuck with him because I am all that he really has, and I love him; and he loves me."

Beatrice once expressed her philosophy of marriage to her daughters: "A marriage is like a tree; sometimes it is in bud; sometimes in blossom; sometimes in leaf, sometimes in fruit; and then sometimes the leaves will all fall off and it will look dead, but if you keep on cultivating the roots, always cultivating the roots, it will come alive again."

Volunteering to teach Sunday school on a military base where the family was stationed, Beatrice knowingly took on an unruly group of older boys who were a trial to the post chaplain. Puzzled by her success with the boys, the chaplain asked for an explanation. Beatrice explained, with some embarrassment, that she had told the boys that if they behaved themselves, learned their lessons, and attended Sunday school for four consecutive weeks, they would be invited to the Patton home for a special treat—to put their finger in the trigger of the revolver that George Patton had used to kill Julio Cardenas, a lieutenant of Pancho Villa, during the punitive expedition in Mexico in 1916.[8]

While Beatrice and her brother, Freddie, were growing up, their mother, a strict Protestant, had permitted them to attend various churches in Boston until they found one with a style of worship they liked. The youngsters eventually settled on a congregational church. Although her husband was a devout, tithing Episcopalian, Beatrice gave her own children the same freedom to choose their religion. She encouraged her daughters to attend every Sunday school on base. Ruth Ellen explained that eventually the girls settled on the Baptist Sunday school for two reasons: "firstly, because it served cocoa and cookies and, secondly, because the Baptist hymns were so great."[9]

Beatrice's religious tolerance was severely tested, however, when Ruth Ellen announced that she had decided to marry Jim Totten.

Patton himself exclaimed, "Goddammit, you can't marry him! He's too short; he's a field artilleryman; and he's a Catholic!" Having indulged his penchant for histrionics, Patton almost immediately dropped his objections to the union, though, and gave Ruth Ellen his blessing. His wife's opposition proved more formidable.

Beatrice, a grandson later explained, fell back on the anti-Catholic prejudices of her Yankee Puritan background when it came to her daughter's marriage. She decided to persuade Lieutenant Totten to become a Protestant. Patton was horrified; religion, anyone's, was no casual calling to him. He threatened to leave Beatrice if she tried to convert Totten. She went ahead, and Totten refused ("What do you think of turncoats?" he asked her), while Patton, in a gesture of protest on Ruth Ellen's behalf, spent most of that night at the post theater, watching a movie three times.

Seeking another ally, Ruth Ellen went to California to see her Aunt Nita. She was stunned when Nita insisted that under no circumstances should Ruth Ellen marry a Catholic. Feeling beaten, she sighed, "I guess that I will never marry. I'll stay home and take care of Ma." These words and the future they foretold provoked an eruption of regret from Nita over her own aborted romances of long ago. She rose from her chair, her face florid. "What?" she shouted, "and be like me? One sacrifice on the altar of family is enough. Go home and marry your young man. I'll attend your wedding if no one else will!"

The wedding took place on July 6, 1940, in the same church where Ruth Ellen's parents had wed. Her mother had come around soon after Nita, a few days before the wedding. Beatrice gave Ruth Ellen a handwritten collection of motherly advice. One tip reflected something that she and her daughter both understood about Patton: "To wish to reform a man is to set yourself above God. Live the best you know, and perhaps one unhappy seeker will see in your behavior the key to his own freedom."[10]

During World War II, Beatrice lived in Green Meadows, Massa-chusetts. She became fixated on saving gasoline, apparently certain that every drop she saved would go straight to her husband's tanks. As a result, she almost never drove her automobile. She did wish to go to church every week, so in good weather she drove a donkey cart four miles into nearby Hamilton. Occasionally Ruth Ellen, dressed in her church clothes, would have to get out and push when they came to a slope in the road. On their fourth Sunday trip, as they began to hitch up the donkey for the return trip home, a wealthy aunt pulled up in her chauffeur-driven Rolls-Royce. She opened the door and called to Beatrice, sitting cross-legged in the cart, "Beatrice, dear, do you think it is *quite* the thing for an Ayer to be riding to church in that—vehicle?" Looking the aunt up and down, Beatrice replied, "Well, Fedy, if our Lord could enter Jerusalem on the rear end of an ass, I don't see why I can't go to church on a donkey cart." With that, Aunt Theodora closed her car door, and the Rolls-Royce "purred splendidly away."[11]

With the outbreak of World War II, Beatrice began speaking before church groups, civic groups, and ladies' lunches. *Life* magazine published an excerpt from one such talk to an officers' wives club:

> There is no career, except that of a minister's wife, in which a woman can be of such a help or detriment to her husband as that of an Army wife. She lives practically at his place of business, and sees his associates daily. Her reputation begins at her first post and sticks to her as closely as her skin until she dies. I have known several able officers to be ruined absolutely by malicious gossipy wives.
>
> I joined the Army in 1910—the piping times of peace. But the older women knew. Before my first child was born

I had seen my husband's bedding roll at the front door, ready to leave if the regiment went to Mexico. Since then, I have seen him off to three wars. He has led troops in battle, been gravely wounded, and has been decorated for extraordinary heroism. Now, I belong to the older generation of Army women who preach, Be happy today. Who knows what tomorrow will hold?

To a radio audience, Beatrice said:

He's always known that some day his country would need him and that he must be ready. He's not only a great student of tactics and history, but he brings the past right into the present and applies it to the situation in hand. When he was in Africa, he used to write me about Hannibal....

He believes that God will help him.... He believes in himself, and he believes in his soldiers. In his battle order before Sicily, he says, "Remember that, as attackers, we have the initiative. We must retain this tremendous advantage by attacking rapidly, viciously, ruthlessly, without rest, however tired, and punching. God is with us. We shall win."[12]

Beatrice once told her daughter Ruth Ellen that Ruth of the Old Testament would have made the perfect patron saint of service wives: "Whither thou goest, I will go; and where thou lodgest, I shall lodge: thy people shall be my people, and thy God my God: Where thou diest, will I die, and there will I be buried: the Lord do so to me, and more also, if aught but death part thee and me."

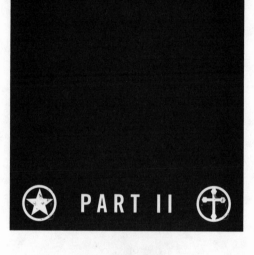

PART II

GUTS

W hile a cadet at West Point, Patton attended a lecture on electricity. The professor displayed an induction coil with a twelve-inch spark, and one of the students asked if it would kill a man if it passed through his hand or arm. The professor invited the inquiring cadet to try it, but his offer was promptly refused. After the lecture, Patton asked if he could try. The professor at first declined, but Patton persisted and the instructor relented. Patton was curious to see how it would feel. "It hardly hurt at all though my arm is still a little stiff," Patton wrote to his then girlfriend, Beatrice Ayer.

Patton was always testing his courage. As a young officer teaching new recruits to fire on a rifle range, he deliberately exposed himself to their gunfire, standing between the targets. When he felt his destiny had eluded him, he tested himself again by setting out on a perilous journey in the Pacific in his boat, the *Arcturus*. His survival assured him that his destiny still awaited him.

Patton recognized that all men, including him, were afraid in combat. In World War I he shook in terror under German machine gun fire. During that same conflict he once stood on a hillside in a game of "chicken" with the future General Douglas MacArthur, seeing who would "blink" first. When Patton instinctively crouched at the explosion of a nearby shell, MacArthur coolly warned him not to worry—"You never hear the one that gets you."

CHAPTER FIVE

PANCHO VILLA

"His dearest wish is realized. He has gone to war."

—NITA PATTON

In 1938, with another world war looming, the Patton family moved to Fort Clark, situated in a desolate stretch of the Texas-Mexico border, where George, now a colonel, assumed command of the Fifth Cavalry. One night the Pattons dined in a restaurant across the border in Piedras Negras, where they encountered a group of Mexican officers. One of the Mexicans kept looking at the Pattons "in a rather pointed way," Ruth Ellen recalled. By the time the Pattons finished their meal, the Mexicans had left. When Patton tried to pay his bill, he was informed that it had already been paid by the general who had just left, the commander of the Coahuila district. The general, moreover, had asked to be remembered to Teniente Patton, whom he had last seen under somewhat different circumstances in 1915. Patton slapped his leg and exclaimed, "I knew I had seen that man before! He was one of Pancho Villa's officers! That goddamn Yaqui shot at me and nearly winged me!"[1]

Pro-democracy forces in Mexico had clashed with federal troops in 1910, sparking a revolution. Mexico had been ruled by Porfirio Diaz, a virtual dictator, since 1876, and the regime was increasingly unpopular. After raising hopes for a free election, Diaz declared himself the winner of an eighth term in office and imprisoned his rival Francisco Madero. After posting bail, Madero fled to the United States, and from San Antonio, Texas, he issued a call to arms against the Diaz regime.

Among the men who would answer Madero's call was José Doroteo Arango Arámbula, better known as Pancho Villa. He claimed to have killed his first man at sixteen (for allegedly raping his sister). Villa had then embarked on a career in horse thievery, banditry, and violence, interspersed with occasional legitimate pursuits. His path changed when he met Abraham Gonzalez, the local representative for Madero. Gonzalez persuaded Villa to fight for the people against the ruling class of hacienda owners. Villa transformed himself into a "social bandit"—a kind of Mexican Robin Hood.

Pancho Villa joined Madero's forces in their first clash with the federals at Cuidad Juárez in Chihuahua in April and May 1911. After two days of fighting, the garrison surrendered, giving the revolutionaries their first victory. A stunned Diaz soon fled to France. Madero became president, only to be betrayed and assassinated. General Victoriano Huerta proclaimed himself provisional president of Mexico. Villa joined the effort to overthrow Huerta. When Huerta ordered the murder of Abraham Gonzalez, Villa's friend and political mentor, Villa's hatred for Huerta became even more intense and personal. The United States supported the anti-Huerta forces, and Huerta fled from office on July 15, 1914.

During this second part of the Mexican Revolution, Pancho Villa had exhibited remarkable ability to organize and lead an army. When he joined the rebellion against Huerta, Villa had only eight men, two pounds of sugar, and five hundred rounds of rifle ammunition. He eventually raised a large army, recruiting both Mexicans and mercenaries, and supplemented his fundraising with forced assessments on hacienda owners and train robberies.

After a string of victories by the anti-Huerta forces, Villa was appointed provincial governor of the state of Chihuahua. He and his one-time ally, Venustiano Carranza, then turned their armies on each other. Despite earlier public expressions of support for Villa, President Woodrow Wilson decided that Carranza was the best hope for stability in Mexico, and the United States recognized him as president.

Villa was enraged by what he perceived to be the Americans' betrayal. Perhaps trying to provoke an American intervention in Mexico that would discredit Carranza's government, Villa and his band of *pistoleros* launched a series of raids across the border, frightening Americans in the border towns of Texas, New Mexico, and Arizona. President Wilson responded to the raids by sending troops to Texas and New Mexico in the spring of 1914. Among them was the Eighth Infantry under the command of Brigadier General John J. Pershing, dispatched from the Presidio in San Francisco to Fort Bliss, near El Paso.

Pershing, derisively known as "Black Jack" because of his earlier command of the all-black Tenth Cavalry, was a veteran of the Indian wars as well as an uprising in the Philippines, and he was now one of the most highly respected officers in the army. He was greeted eagerly by the population of El Paso, who viewed him as their savior from Pancho Villa. Lean and ramrod straight, Pershing was a stern leader and a strict disciplinarian. When provoked to anger, he could produce an icy glare that struck fear into even his veteran troopers. Pershing confidently prepared to undertake the mission of taking the fight to the Mexican bandits.

After a year at Fort Bliss, Pershing decided to have his wife and four children join him at his new quarters. The arrangements for the move were almost complete when, on August 27, 1915, a fire raced through the Pershings' quarters at the Presidio, killing the general's wife and three daughters. Only his six-year-old son survived. Among the many messages of condolence Pershing received was one signed "Fransciso (Pancho) Villa."

A devastated Pershing returned from his family's funerals with his son and sister, Mae, and resumed his duties. George Patton arrived at Fort Bliss shortly thereafter, while Beatrice and the children remained behind in Massachusetts to await word on living quarters. Patton was immediately enchanted by the romantically rugged Wild West. The sprawling landscape was populated by Indians, Texas Rangers, Mexican outlaws, and frontier women, some of questionable virtue. "I would not miss this for the world," he wrote to his wife. "I guess there are few places like it left."[2]

In a letter to his Aunt Nannie, Patton described a panther hunter he had met. "He was very dark and commented on it. Saying 'Damn it a fellow took me for a Mex and I had to shoot him three times before he believed I was white.' This impressed me very much and I assured him that he was the whitest man I ever had seen."[3] Patton got on well with the larger-than-life Texans: "I usually do with that sort of people."

During his time in Texas Patton adopted what became two of his trademarks. A Texas Ranger named Colonel Sterling gave him a .45 caliber Colt single-action revolver, model 1873, which he carried the rest of his life. Patton later had the walnut grips replaced with ivory— one side of the handle was etched with an eagle, the other sported his initials set in black enamel. Sterling—"a rodeo peacock in tassels and spurs and silver shirt studs"—displayed a sartorial audacity that Patton would come to imitate.[4] Patton also began to copy an old rancher's use of the most shocking profanities. Taking note of the impression that the rancher made with his colorful language, Patton employed a similar means of communication with his troops, raising it to an art form.

Beatrice joined her husband at Fort Bliss in December 1915, leaving the children behind with her parents. Soon after her arrival, the Pattons attended a dinner party of local ranchers and their wives at a hotel near Sierra Blanca. During coffee, a gun discharged, and everyone dived to the floor. When it was clear that there would be no further gun fire, the party broke up. Driving home, Patton crashed headlong into a cattle gate without making any effort to brake. Beatrice, shaken by the collision, was surprised to see tears streaming down her husband's face. "You don't give a damn about me!" he cried. "That was *my* pistol that went off. I might have been killed, and you didn't even ask if I was okay!" Patton had adopted the somewhat dangerous local custom of carrying a pistol in his waistband. Beatrice assured her uncertain husband of her love, but the incident betrayed a lifelong insecurity that Patton always felt with his wife. Despite her complete devotion to him, he always approached his wife like a suitor uncertain of his chances.

In February 1916, Nita Patton traveled from California to visit her brother and sister-in-law at Fort Bliss. Though she enjoyed the attention of a number of officers, the twenty-eight-year-old Nita was increasingly worried about her single status. When she met the recently widowed post commander, General Pershing, she was immediately taken with him. "He is awfully good-looking and entertaining—and is sort of historical, too," she noted.[5] Soon it became apparent that the fifty-five-year old Pershing was interested in her.

Patton himself was conflicted about the budding romance between Pershing and his sister. Emotionally close to his sibling, he understood her concern that she might never find a life partner. But as much as he enjoyed the visibility and social connection with his commander, he was also concerned, especially if they should marry, that his own achievements would be diminished by the suspicion that his standing was the result of his sister's bond with Pershing. Nita and Pershing became secretly engaged in 1917, but the engagement did not survive the First World War. Nita never married, and Pershing died a widower.

Pancho Villa launched a campaign of revenge against the United States in January 1916. At Santa Ysabel, sixteen American mining engineers were abducted from a train and executed. Despite the public outrage, the U.S. took no action. Two months later Villa and perhaps five hundred of his men moved north from Sonora, leaving a wake of violence and death. They kidnapped an American woman for nine days after killing her husband. Others were raped, brutalized, and strangled.

Villa's band struck Columbus, New Mexico, early on the morning of March 9, indiscriminately burning, looting, and killing. Eighteen Americans—eight soldiers and ten civilians—were killed in the raid. An army lieutenant who was in Columbus that day, John Lucas, set up machine guns in the center of town and fired on the attackers. His quick actions inflicted heavy casualties, killing eighty of them and causing them to retreat back to Mexico. But Villa had achieved his intended goal of arousing the ire of the United States and provoking retaliation.

News of the raid reached Fort Bliss on March 8. Two days later a distraught Patton learned that his unit, the Eighth Cavalry, would not be part of the Punitive Expedition into Mexico. He silently cursed his overweight commander, certain that he had been deemed unfit for field duty. "There should be a law killing fat colonels on sight," he bitterly complained.[6] But Patton was determined not to miss his first opportunity to go to war. He sought to transfer out of his unit and to persuade Pershing to take him along as his aide-de-camp.

Patton appealed to two of Pershing's aides, requesting a position on the general's staff. When Pershing learned of Patton's inquiries, he telephoned him to ask if it were true that he sought to accompany the expedition. Patton excitedly responded yes but was discouraged by Pershing's perfunctory reply: "I'll see what I can do." That evening, Patton arrived unannounced at Pershing's quarters to make his case in person. He promised to perform any task, no matter how menial, if he could go along. Patton also insisted that he was good at handling newspaper reporters—a boast on which certain episodes later in his career would cast an ironic light. Skeptical, Pershing responded, "Everyone wants to go. Why should I favor you?" A brash Patton shot back, "Because I want to go more than anyone else." Patton's impertinence went over poorly with Pershing, a man of tightly controlled emotions. He looked at the young officer coldly—"That will do."

The next morning, however, Pershing telephoned Patton. "Lieutenant Patton, how soon can you be ready?" Always the optimist, Patton had already packed his gear. Right away, he said. "I'll be God Damned. You are appointed Aide."[7] Three years later, Pershing revealed to Patton why he had accepted him on the expedition. Pershing was a lieutenant and an instructor at West Point when the Spanish-American War broke out in 1898. It was army policy that no instructors leave their positions to go fight. When he had exhausted all the standard channels for getting an exception, Pershing went AWOL to Washington where, displaying brashness similar to Patton's, he secured a detail to Cuba.[8] It is also likely, however, that Pershing's growing attraction to Patton's sister also played a role in the selection of the commander's aide-de-camp.

Pershing was perhaps the most important mentor of Patton's military career. He saw a lot of himself in the eager young officer, and he was flattered by Patton's at times comical emulation. Both men were consummate professionals, and Pershing read Patton's frequent papers on tactics with interest, providing careful critiques. When time allowed, the two men would go on horseback rides into the countryside. As D'Este notes:

> Pershing's influence on young Patton cannot be overemphasized. He was the very model of a military commander, whose ideas of duty and discipline meshed perfectly with

Patton's own conception. Pershing would not brook disorder or sloppiness of mind or person or billet, and he was a superb organizer of troops. He even possessed the same short-fused temper as Patton.... In Pershing [Patton] had at last found the perfect example of a senior commander, whom he would later successfully emulate, refining to his own lofty standards what he had learned.[9]

Patton came to idolize Pershing and his style of leadership. In a personal memoir of Pershing, Patton wrote, "General Pershing knew to the minutest detail each of the subjects in which he demanded practice and by his physical presence and personal example and explanation insured himself that they were correctly carried out."[10] Pershing eschewed the trappings of rank, and despite the cold, rain, sleet, or wind in the Sierra Madres, he slept on the ground from March to May without a tent. "No frost or snow," Patton noted, "prevented his daily shave."[11]

Orders came from Washington for the Punitive Expedition to cross the border by March 15. There was public jubilation over the military action in response to Villa's strikes. Patton, however, took a sober view of the expedition's chances:

I think that we will have much more of a party than many think as Villa's men at Columbus fought well and... [Mexico is] very bad [terrain] for regular troops. There are no roads and no maps and no water for the first 100 miles. If we can induce him to fight it will be all right but if he breaks up [his force] it will be bad, especially if we have Carranza on our rear. They can't beat us but they will kill a lot of us. Not me though.[12]

Pershing's mission, to catch Pancho Villa, was practically impossible. The expedition faced the problems that always accompany a conventional force's pursuit of non-conventional forces in their native lands. They were surrounded by a hostile local population, which was friendly or at least indifferent to the insurgents. They presented a large, slowly moving target to a more agile adversary. And unless the enemy decided to present himself for battle, it was impossible for the Americans to inflict losses on him.

The calculus of guerrilla warfare, which favors the insurgents, was not the only problem Pershing faced. The terrain of northern Mexico is unforgiving, a vast desert dominated by the Sierra Madres, a chain of peaks ten to twelve thousand feet high with deep canyons providing an excellent refuge for anyone seeking to hide. The primitive network of roads consisted mostly of dirt trails that became muddy traps when it rained. Pershing also faced the monumental logistical challenge of resupplying his force every day as it moved farther away from its base in the United States.

Six aircraft—the dangerously unstable Curtiss JN-2 "Jennies"— were Pershing's means of communication with his widely scattered forces. They were flown by the brave but inexperienced pioneers of the First Aero Squadron. The Jennies had all crashed within a month.[13] The experience highlighted, however, the potential for the use of aircraft for reconnaissance and intelligence gathering. And Patton himself became a firm believer in the use of airpower in coordination with tanks and ground troops, as he would show in World War II.

Just as he had hoped, the expedition provided opportunities for Patton to test his courage. An urgent message had to be delivered to the Eleventh Cavalry, whose whereabouts to the south were only vaguely ascertained. Patton volunteered. When Pershing resisted sending his aide on the dangerous mission, Patton persisted until the commander relented. It was like looking for "a needle in a haystack," recalled Patton. "As I started the General shook me warmly by the hand saying, 'Be careful, there are lots of Villistas.' Then still holding my hand he said, 'But remember, Patton, if you don't deliver that message don't come back.' It was delivered."[14]

In the spring of 1916, the Punitive Expedition motored through the Mexican wilderness. Pershing's entourage consisted of only three open-air automobiles manned by fifteen men carrying only nine rifles. Patton was in the lead car. As the convoy traversed unmapped and dangerous territory, an armed Mexican suddenly appeared in the headlight. A "veritable army seemed to lurk" in the shadows. Patton rushed forward, his heart pounding in his chest, and began speaking in halting Spanish. Uncertain whether they were friend or foe and fearing that an ambush was about to wipe them out, Patton exaggerated his force's size, claiming that they were the advance guard of an automobile regiment. An angry Pershing then presented himself and demanded to know why in the hell he was being stopped. Patton later wrote, "The commanding presence of the General, and his utter disregard of danger over-awed the Mexicans and we went on, though personally it was more than a mile before I ceased feeling bullets entering my back." Patton's fears appeared to be well-founded when, two hours later, another convoy of three trucks was attacked, apparently by the same Mexicans. "Fortune favors the bold," Patton thought to himself when he heard of the later incident.[15]

The commander of Pancho Villa's personal bodyguards, General Julio Cardenas, was believed to be hiding somewhere near Rubio. Pershing ordered that search operations in the vicinity of Rubio be intensified. Predictably, Patton sought a role in the manhunt for Cardenas and pestered Pershing to allow him to participate until the general relented. As a result, Patton was temporarily assigned to First Lieutenant Innis Palmer Swift's Troop C, Thirteenth Cavalry.[16] The target of the search was the San Miguelito Ranch, thought to be the home of the Cardenas family. Villa might escape, but Patton hoped that they could snare one of his most trusted subordinates.

A search of the house yielded nothing, but the Americans had noticed several armed Mexicans heading for the nearby hills as they approached. A subsequent search of the area by Patton's new detail uncovered Cardenas's wife, baby, and uncle. Patton seemed to believe that Cardenas was still in the area and suspected that he would be drawn back to San Miguelito to visit his family. He could not resist testing his hunch and his courage by seeking a confrontation with the Villista.

His opportunity came on May 14, when Pershing sent him out with ten soldiers from the Sixth Infantry Regiment and two civilian guides in three automobiles to purchase corn to feed his troops. When they arrived in Rubio, a group of about sixty Mexicans drew their attention. The men were unarmed, but one of Patton's guides, a former Villa compatriot named E. L. Holmdahl, recognized several of them. As Patton purchased grain for the horses, he plotted an attack to test his hunch about Cardenas—he would launch a raid on San Miguelito before anyone in Rubio had a chance to warn the unsuspecting Villistas.

Braced for battle, Patton and his troops raced to Cardenas's uncle's ranch in Saltillo, but found no trace of Cardenas. They next targeted the Cardenas hacienda in San Miguelito, six miles to the north. It was there at high noon, appropriately enough, that Patton engaged in a shootout with Cardenas and his band. Patton described the encounter in a written report:

> About a mile and a half south of the house the ground is lower than the house. And one cannot be seen until topping the rise. As soon as I came over this, I made my car go at full speed and went on past the house…. [F]our men were seen skinning a cow in the front. One of these men ran to the house and at once returned and went on with his work. I stopped my car northwest of the house and the other two southwest of it. I jumped out carrying my rifle in my left hand [and] hurried around to the big arched door leading into the patio…. I rounded the corner and walked about halfway to the gate. When I was fifteen yards from the gate three armed men dashed out on horseback, and started around the southeast corner.

So schooled was I not to shoot, that I merely drew my pistol and waited to see what would happen[17]. . . . When they got to the corner they saw my men coming that way and turned back and all three shot at me. One bullet threw gravel on me. I fired back with my new pistol five times. Then my men came around the corner and started to shoot. I did not know who was in the house. There were a lot of windows only a few feet from our right side. Just as I got around the corner three bullets hit about seven feet from the ground and put adobe [chips] all over me.[18]

Patton had approached the hacienda running, while bobbing and weaving to dodge anyone potentially taking aim at him. When three riders dashed out of the gate, Patton shouted, "Halt!" to no effect. As Patton, Holmdahl, and two soldiers reloaded behind the north wall of the hacienda, the three Mexicans, one of whom was wounded, were trapped inside the courtyard, their escape routes cut off by troops Patton had ordered to the southeast and the southwest. "I reloaded my pistol and started back when I saw a man on a horse come right in front of me. I started to shoot at him but remembered that Dave Allison had always said to shoot at the horse of an escaping man and I did so, and broke the horse's hip. He fell on his rider and as it was only about ten yards, we all hit him. He crumpled up."[19]

In the confusion, a second Mexican eluded the Americans. He was not detected until he was nearly a hundred yards east of the hacienda. Just as he seemed likely to escape, he was caught in a hail of rifle fire and pitched forward, dead. Patton had fired at him three or four times with his rifle, as had four or five of his soldiers. Two of the three Mexicans were now dead.

Uncertain how many of Villa's militiamen might be present, Patton clambered onto the dirt roof of the hacienda to prevent potential enemies from using a parapet there as a firing position. The roof, however, gave way beneath his feet, and Patton found himself dangling from his armpits. Aware that he was dangerously exposed to anyone inside the building, he scrambled to pull himself back onto the roof.

At the same time, Holmdahl was covering the front door and spotted a man running from a gate in the southwest corner toward the nearby fields: "He was dropped at about two hundred yards and held up his hand in a token of surrender but as Holmdahl approached him he drew his pistol and fired at Holmdahl who then killed him."

Conducting a room-by-room search of the house, Patton and his men encountered Cardenas's mother and wife, the latter rocking an infant daughter in her arms. The two women looked at Patton and his men in stony silence. Another room was protected by a padlocked door. Patton blasted the lock away with his gun and discovered several cowering women inside. One of them began praying to God to save their souls and bring his wrath upon the evil Americans.

Although it was impossible during the shootout to determine if Cardenas himself had been killed, in the aftermath Patton noted that one of the horses belonged to Cardenas and bore his silver saddle and saber. One of the Mexican skinners then identified Cardenas's corpse. He had been wounded by Patton as the three riders were driven back into the courtyard. He was the last man killed, finally executed by Holmdahl while attempting to flee the hacienda. An examination of his belts of ammunition cartridges revealed that he had fired thirty-five rounds before he died. The two other dead men were an unnamed Villista captain and private.

Patton and his men strapped the bodies to the hoods of their automobiles like animal carcasses. As they prepared to depart, they were approached by dozens of Villistas on horseback. Some shots were exchanged while the Americans retreated hastily to Rubio. Patton ordered the telephone wires cut to interfere with anyone planning an ambush ahead.

At four o'clock, approximately four hours after the hostilities had commenced, the men returned to Pershing's field headquarters with their grisly trophies. Patton's shootout created an instant sensation in the press back in the United States, including a graphic account in the *New York Times* that branded Patton the "Bandit Killer."

When Patton wrote to his wife about the encounter, he told her that "I have always expected to be scared but was not nor was I excited. I was afraid they would get away. I never heard a bullet but some say that you do not at such close range. I wondered a little at first that I was not hit, they were so close.... You are probably wondering if my conscience hurts me for killing a man it does not. I feel about it as I did when I got my swordfish, surprised at my luck."[20]

Patton's daughter Ruth Ellen recalled how the family's connection with Pancho Villa was renewed many years after:

> Forty-eight years later, when my husband was stationed at Fort Sill, Oklahoma, the Mexican General Staff came for their biannual visit.... The last night we were there, we had a large formal dinner.... There was a lot of whispering... and, finally... [a] little old [Mexican] general got up, and... said, "I weesh to toast not only thees lady and her fine hoosband, but to her fader also, I knowed him well!" I said, in surprise: "You knew my father?"
>
> The rest of the Mexicans began to laugh.... "Oh yees, I knowed your fader well. I shoot at him many times... I was weeth Pancho Villa!"[21]

CHAPTER SIX

WORLD WAR I

"It is time for another Patton to die."

—PATTON BEFORE HIS WOUNDING AT CHEPPY

September 26, 1918

Patton had once again disobeyed orders to remain at his command post. Two weeks earlier, on the night before the offensive of Saint-Mihiel, Patton's commanding officer, Brigadier General Samuel D. Rockenbach, had carefully instructed him: "There is no question of personal courage in this war; it is a business proposition where every man must be in his place and performing his part. Keep control of your reserve and supply, you have no business in a tank and I give you the order not to go into this fight in a tank." Patton chose to interpret his orders literally—he did not to go into battle *in* a tank. He went *on top of* a tank.[1]

Marshall Ferdinand Foch, the French supreme commander of the Allied armies, had ordered the U.S. First Army to shift its operations from Saint-Mihiel to the Meuse-Argonne. Patton's First Tank Brigade was slated to play an important role in an offensive to be launched there on September 26, and Patton sensed that the battle would be tough. The territory was a thousand feet above sea level and carved with deep ravines and bluffs. Its German defenders enjoyed a power-ful advantage, which they had skillfully exploited by establishing three defensive belts in front of the main Hindenburg line. On the right flank of the position was another barrier, the Meuse River. The First Army's chief of staff, Brigadier General Hugh A. Drum, called the enemy position "the most ideal defensive terrain I have ever seen or read about."[2] Because of its formidable defenses, the sector had been largely inactive. Parties of soldiers from both sides casually hunted squirrels in no man's land, observed only by the uniformed skeletons of soldiers killed four years earlier.[3] The German defenses along the twenty-four-mile front were lightly manned with only five divisions.

Before the battle, in order to avoid trouble with his commander, Patton made special preparations to maintain communications with Rockenbach. On the morning of September 26, he assembled his recon-naissance officer, his signal officer, twelve enlisted runners, a number of carrier pigeons, field telephones, and a large quantity of telephone wire.[4] At 2:30 in the morning, the Allied artillery barrage began pum-meling the German position. In the three hours preceding the attack, twenty-eight hundred Allied guns expended more ammunition than both the Union and Confederate forces fired during the entire four years of the American Civil War.[5] Patton offered up a prayer of thanks that he was not at the receiving end of the powerful barrage.[6]

At 5:30 a.m., under the cover of dense fog, the Americans had advanced from the relative safety of their muddy trenches into the German lines. For the first hour, Patton resisted the impulse to go forward with his men, but at 6:30 he led his command group on, closely following the tracks of his leading tank companies. The American artillery was firing smoke shells, which, combined with the fog, limited vision to a mere ten feet and forced Patton to navigate the treacherous landscape with a hand-held compass.

By ten o'clock, Patton and his men had advanced to a crossroads on the southern edge of Cheppy. A few minutes later, when the fog began to lift, Patton discovered that he had advanced beyond his own tanks, many of which were now entangled in a trench barrier over a hundred yards to his rear.[7] As the protective shield of fog lifted, Patton and his troops were subjected to withering fire from all directions. The defending Germans had pre-positioned at least twenty-five machine gun nests to protect the town.

The capture of Cheppy was an objective for the Thirty-fifth Division, a unit comprising National Guardsmen from Kansas and Missouri, on the first day of the offensive. Under the intense German fire, the division's inexperienced soldiers panicked, became lost, or fled back to friendly lines. The troops were now leaderless. When Patton discovered that he was the only officer, he ordered the soldiers to remain with him. Eventually he gathered several hundred scared doughboys like a mother hen gathering up scattered chicks. Twice the men started to run, but Patton hollered at them to stay put.

Seeing his tanks behind him, Patton sent a succession of soldiers to bring them up to his position. When the men failed to return, Patton himself ran down the hill to see what the delay was. He discovered that the lead tank had become trapped, the lumbering metal beast unable to hurl itself across an unusually wide trench. The crewmen were frantically digging to free the tank, but they frequently had to take cover from machine gun fire. Patton, seeing soldiers cowering in the trenches while their comrades exposed themselves to fire, became enraged. He and Captain Matthew English, the commander of the tank group, removed the picks and shovels strapped to the side of their other tanks and handed them out to the soldiers hiding in the trenches. Patton ordered the men to ignore the bullets and start digging.

A German spotter plane then appeared overhead, lazily circling the Americans' position and directing enemy fire on the inviting target of stranded tanks, crewmen, and soldiers. As fresh gunfire erupted, all the soldiers but Patton leapt back into the security of the trench. The men implored Patton to escape from the Germans' fire, but he refused to budge. "To hell with them—they can't hit me!" Several soldiers were struck down, but Patton refused to take cover. When at last the men got five tanks across the breach, Patton exhorted them to advance again, yelling and cursing and waving his walking stick. About a hundred and fifty doughboys followed him, but when they arrived at the crest of the hill, the onslaught of gunfire forced them all to the ground, hugging it for protection.

The intensity from the German machine guns reminded Patton of a lawnmower cutting the grass at his Lake Vineyard home in California. Suddenly desperation and fear stripped away Patton's veneer of bravado, and he began to shake with terror.[8] He wanted to run. He lifted his face up from the dirt, gazed out over the German lines, and then lifted his eyes up to the clouds—and saw faces. He blinked, then squinted his eyes, but the faces remained. They were faces of his ancestors. There was General Hugh Mercer, mortally wounded at the battle of Princeton in the Revolutionary War. There was his grandfather Colonel George Patton, killed at Winchester in the Civil War; and Colonel Waller Tazewell Patton, who died from wounds received at Gettysburg. There were other faces and different uniforms, dimmer in the distance, but with the same family resemblance. All the faces looked at Patton impersonally, as if waiting for him to join them.

Patton seemed to understand instinctively that the faces were beckoning him to his destiny. He immediately became calm, shaking off his tremors of fear. "It is time for another Patton to die," he said aloud. He stood up, grabbed his walking stick, and turned to the soldiers behind him. "Who is with me?" he yelled. Patton headed back out into the enemy fire, certain of meeting death. Of the hundred and fifty soldiers, only six followed him, one of whom was his orderly, Private Joseph Angelo. Soon only two men were standing—Patton and Angelo. The others lay dead or wounded. As he charged forward, Patton eerily saw himself as a small, detached figure on the battlefield, watched all the time from a cloud by his Confederate kinsmen and his Virginia grandfather.[9]

As he came closer to the German lines, Patton was hit. He staggered forward a few steps before collapsing. Angelo leaped to Patton's side to see what was wrong. He dragged his commander to a shallow crater and bandaged his wound, which was bleeding profusely, while the Germans kept firing at their position. Angelo knew that Patton had been gravely wounded and needed medical attention. But the two men were caught in enemy crossfire, and rescuing Patton seemed impossible.

He had now achieved his destiny, Patton thought, joining the warrior kinsmen who had gone before. He had not failed them. He had shown his courage and faced his fears. He was dying, but he had no fear of death. He was comforted by his unshakeable faith, a faith he had held since childhood and that he had carefully nurtured every day since.

As he lay bleeding in a bomb crater, Patton ordered Angelo to return to the tanks and point out the location of the machine gun nests. After two hours, Patton's tankers and the 138th Regiment of the Thirty-fifth Division subdued the Germans and seized the village of Cheppy. Patton was carried off to an ambulance. Before heading to the field hospital, he insisted that the ambulance driver take him to the headquarters of the Thirty-fifth Division, where he began to dictate a report on the situation at the battle front. In his weakened state, however, the effort proved too strenuous, and Patton lapsed into unconsciousness. Unable to offer further protest, he was taken to an evacuation hospital behind the lines.

When a doctor examined the wound, he could not understand how the bullet had traversed Patton's body without crippling him for life. Though the doctor could not run a probe without striking the hip joint, sciatic nerve, or a major artery, the bullet, miraculously, had touched none of them.[10] Patton suffered little pain and could soon walk perfectly, but the boredom and inactivity of his confinement to a hospital bed left him with mild depression. It did not help that he looked out on a cemetery, where he watched people being buried all day long. A French colonel came by Patton's bedside to pay his regards. "I am glad you were only wounded. You are one of those gallant men who always get killed," he said. The Frenchman then warned, "But you will get it yet."[11]

The Argonne Forest was largely secured by mid-October, while Patton was still recovering. American casualties exceeded 122,000 men—26,277 killed and 95,786 wounded. Patton despaired over having missed the remaining fighting in the offensive. He eventually bribed an orderly, got himself a car, and deserted the hospital. He arrived in Verdun on his thirty-third birthday, November 11, 1918.[12] But later that morning—at the eleventh hour of the eleventh day of the eleventh month—the guns on the Western Front fell silent. The Germans had asked for an armistice. The most violent conflict in history up to that time was over.

Patton learned an important lesson from the battle of the Argonne Forest. Though the Allies had reduced the effectiveness of their tanks by dispersing them, a concentration of armor at carefully chosen points would have been decisive. The young officer began to see the power of tank combat as a fluid form of maneuver warfare. This idea would germinate for over two decades until Patton decisively deployed tanks in the greatest battle America has ever fought.

He was to learn another, more painful lesson—that for George S. Patton Jr., peace was a more difficult assignment than war.

CHAPTER SEVEN

TANKS

"The only thing harder than getting a new idea into the military mind is to get an old one out."

—B. H. LIDDELL HART

I n the twenty years between the end of World War I and the Nazi invasion of Poland, there was a dramatic struggle within the United States Army over the role of the tank. The powerful new mechanized weapon had proved its value in the Great War, but traditionalists saw it as merely a complement to the infantry, aiding what they saw as the main objective, getting the troops across "no man's land." Others saw the tank as a more powerful version of the cavalry, a means of delivering a swift blow to the enemy by outflanking its forces and attacking its rear. The tank's proponents argued that it deserved to be independent from the infantry, in the same way that artillery was. This idea was odious to the traditionalists. The debate was also not merely an intellectual exchange. Those who promoted the mechanized form of warfare knew that by challenging the established order they were risking their own careers. Advancement in the reduced peacetime army was painfully slow, and anyone seen as a threat to the primacy of the infantry might be sidelined, court-martialed, or strongly encouraged to exit the service.

Patton's return from the conflict in Europe was marked by the "hangover" of war familiar to many veterans. The sudden transition from the highly-charged experience of combat, where one is commanding men in life-or-death situations, to domestic tranquility can be jarring and difficult. Patton felt the loss of camaraderie and sense of purpose. He also faced uncertainty about his career in peacetime. For a man driven by a belief in his own destiny to lead troops in warfare, peace was more frightening than war. Making the situation even more painful, it was the practice in the U.S. Army to reduce returning officers to the rank they held before the war. Patton lost his rank of colonel and reverted to captain.

During these interwar years, Patton met another officer whose destiny would be bound up with his own. In the autumn of 1919, he was introduced to Dwight David Eisenhower, known to his friends as Ike. Both men were commanding tank units. Eisenhower had not been sent off to France during the war but had established and run the largest tank training center in the United States—Camp Colt, at Gettysburg, Pennsylvania. In many ways Patton and Eisenhower were strikingly different. Patton could be painfully direct. At times he was an insufferable egotist, and he often sought to intimidate with a well-practiced scowl. His wealthy background allowed him to enjoy an upper-crust way of life in a hardscrabble army. Eisenhower was self-effacing and came from dirt-poor beginnings. His disarming smile charmed everyone who met him. Those who knew both men at this early stage of their military careers had the feeling that George Patton would achieve greatness. Eisenhower, on the other hand, was usually underrated, his easygoing manner masking a burning ambition. Few would have predicted that Eisenhower would become the most brilliant star of the West Point class of 1915—the "class the stars fell on."[1]

While Eisenhower was attending the army's Command and General Staff College from 1925 to 1926 at Fort Leavenworth, Patton sent him his own very detailed notes from the course. Eisenhower graduated first in his class, presumably with some help from his friend's insights and notebook. Patton sent Ike a congratulatory note, remarking that while he was pleased to think that his notes had been of some assistance, "I feel sure that you would have done as well without them." It is likely, though, that Patton felt that his notes were the primary reason for Eisenhower's success at the college.

Years later, recalling his relationship with Patton, Eisenhower wrote, "From the beginning he and I got along famously. Both of us were students of current military doctrine. Part of our passion was our belief in tanks—a belief derided at the time by others."[2] The two men shared a detailed knowledge of the mechanical workings of tanks and an appreciation of their potential strategic uses beyond mere assistance to the infantry.

There was a massive and rapid demobilization of the United States Army at the end of the World War I. By June 1920, the regular army was reduced to only 130,000 men. The American public embraced a pacifism inspired by a vision of the future in which war was a relic of the barbaric past. The League of Nations, which emerged from "the war to end all wars," embodying President Woodrow Wilson's idealistic hopes for international understanding, would peacefully settle future disputes among nations. America settled into a period of innocence and isolation. In 1922 the United States military ranked seventeenth in size among nations with a standing army.

Patton decried this national mood and the dismantling of the army in a letter to his sister dated October 18, 1919:

The United States in general and the army in particular is in a hell of a mess and there seems to be no end to it.... We disregard the lessons of History—The red fate of Carthage; the Rome of shame under the Praetorian guard—and we

go on regardless of the VITAL necessity of trained patriotism—HIRING an army…. Even the most enlightened of
our politicians are blind and mad with self delusion. They
believe what they wish may occur not what history teaches
will happen.[3]

In this eviscerated post-war army, trying to build support for the
tank proved an impossible task. The leadership had no interest in
making room for a new weapon in the shrunken army. Nor was there
any enthusiasm in Congress, given the country's isolationist mood,
for appropriating funds for the military. In 1933 General Douglas
MacArthur noted that the few tanks that the army had were "completely useless for employment against any modern unit on the battlefield."[4]

Like their fellow junior officers, Patton and Eisenhower suffered
post-war reductions in rank, deplorable living conditions, and miser-
able pay. They both contemplated leaving the service, but they both
stuck it out, just as a later generation of officers, in the post-Vietnam
era—men like Norman Schwarzkopf and Colin Powell—would again
rebuild the army into the world's greatest military force. A passionate
belief in the crucial role that tanks could play in the future and the
will to make it happen seemed to sustain both men during this period.
"George and I and a group of young officers thought… [t]anks could
have a more valuable and more spectacular role. We believed…that
they should attack by surprise and mass…. We wanted speed, reliability and firepower."[5]

The two men once took a tank completely apart, down to the nuts
and bolts, and reassembled it, apparently to satisfy their curiosity and
to understand every detail of its intricate assembly. Over endless din-
ners and drinks they would debate and discuss tank tactics and strategy, expanding their discussions to include a small but growing circle
of like-minded men. Winning converts was not easy, but Patton and
Eisenhower were zealots.

Patton arranged for a demonstration of the Christie M1919 tank at Fort Meade in Maryland and persuaded seven general officers from the War Department to attend. Also in attendance were members of the Congressional Military Affairs Committee and members of the Patton family, including Beatrice and her younger brother, Frederick Ayer Jr. Patton began with a brief lecture on the tank's impressive capabilities—it could cruise over sand at thirty miles per hour, penetrate buildings, and crush trees. Patton invited the generals to take the tank on a trial run. When no one accepted his offer, Patton, ever the showman, turned to his wife. "All right, Bea, you demonstrate it!" Mrs. Patton drove the vehicle around the field with perfect skill. When she brought the primitive tank back in front of the visitors, Patton once again invited his guests to take a ride. "You see, gentlemen, how easy it is to handle? Now who would like to make a try?" Instead of the enthusiastic reception Patton had hoped for, there was merely an embarrassing silence. "Thanks, Major Patton, we have seen enough," one general said, ending the demonstration.[6] A congressman approached Patton and said, "It's a beautiful tank, Georgie. Certainly the best we've seen. But we're not going to buy it, you know. I doubt we would even if it were driven up the steps of the Capitol, and loaded with votes."[7]

In September 1919 Patton was selected for the Tank Corps Technical Board of Officers, which studied ways to improve the new armored vehicles. The board met frequently, wrestling with ways to increase the reliability, safety, and lethality of the tank. It was important if not thrilling work. If the tank were to survive against its many enemies, it would need to overcome legitimate questions about its performance and dependability in battle. The board toiled away on the mundane details of tank design. "The members visited repair shops, studied preventive maintenance, recommended changes in the ammunition storage system, the driver's location, the engine, the eyeslits, the foot accelerator, the ground clearance of the axles, the movable roof, the pistol ports, the antiaircraft protection, the seat suspension, the small-arms ammunition racks, and the placement of tools."[8]

Patton threw himself into improving the tank's technical capabilities with his trademark enthusiasm and energy. Evaluations prepared by the Tank Corps commander's office noted that Patton's work as a board member was "well performed." The deputy commander noted that Patton "is enthusiastic about any work he has to do and will accomplish results." He rated Patton as superior in energy, endurance, and initiative. The chief of the Tank Corps was Samuel D. Rockenbach, Patton's commander in World War I. He regarded Patton as "intelligent, active and gallant. Possessing great dash and courage." He rated Patton as superior in all categories except for "judgment and common sense," where he rated Patton above average. The deputy commander of the Tank Corps gave Patton the lower mark of average in the same category.

Another of Patton's recent superiors, Major General J. W. McAndrew, who was commandant of the tank school at Langres, France, during the war, wrote, "Patton is an exceptionally fine soldier and has demonstrated his ability in the field. He is an unusually efficient leader of men in action, and his great usefulness lies in that direction rather than in General Staff Work." He rated Patton superior in all categories, again with the exception of "judgment and common sense," for which he rated Patton above average. The consistent theme of these evaluations is that everyone who worked with Patton appreciated his energy, intelligence, and capacity for hard work. At the same time, his enthusiasm seemed to cloud his judgment, and his interactions with others could be somewhat off-key.[9]

Both Patton and Eisenhower authored essays and articles advocating the further development of the tank and arguing that its speed and firepower could be decisive in a future war. Tanks could outflank an enemy position or tear open gaping holes in the front lines, precipitating the collapse of the enemy's army. They also argued that the tank corps should be separate from the infantry. Patton's and Eisenhower's new doctrine, which threatened the army's powers that be, was politically dangerous, to say the least. It challenged the primacy of the infantry and upset the accepted doctrine of land warfare.

In the autumn of 1920, Eisenhower was ordered to Washington for a meeting with the chief of infantry. He was warned that his views were wrong and dangerous, and he was bluntly told to keep them to himself. He was threatened with a court-martial should he publish anything incompatible with accepted infantry doctrine. This chilling message was not an idle threat. In 1925 General Billy Mitchell was court-martialed for insubordination for publicly advocating an independent air corps. In the minds of the U.S. Army's senior commanders, wars were won by infantry charging the enemy en masse. The military doctrine of the time scorned attempts at maneuvering and outflanking the enemy. This was a classic case of the tendency of generals to fight the last war—especially if they had won it. As the British military strategist B. H. Liddell Hart archly commented, "The only thing harder than getting a new idea into the military mind is to get an old one out."

Hopes for an independent armored branch suffered a blow in 1919 when the most respected military figure of the time, General John J. Pershing, testified before Congress that the Tank Corps "should not be a large organization" and should be placed "under the Chief of Infantry as an adjunct of that arm."[10] Proponents of the tank were crushed on the most important battlefield—Congressional appropriations. In 1920 appropriations for tanks amounted to exactly five hundred dollars.[11]

Patton and Eisenhower conducted a delicate balancing act during this period. Both men believed deeply in the future of armored warfare, but neither was willing to sacrifice his career in the manner of Billy Mitchell. Instead, they retreated and waged a sort of guerrilla campaign to promote interest in tanks by proselytizing with other officers. In written papers and articles, however, both men disingenuously upheld the primacy of the infantry. While a student at the Command and General Staff College, Eisenhower wrote that it was "apparent that tanks can never take over the mission of the infantry, no matter to what degree developed."[12]

After reading *Tanks in the Great War* by British Colonel J. F. C. Fuller, Patton typed seven single-spaced pages of notes, lamenting, "Gun powder rendered armour carried by men useless but it took from the end of the 12th to the beginning of the 14th century for this fact to percolate. Will it take a similar period to show the futility of unarmoured men against armoured machines? Probably."

Patton also noted that Leonardo da Vinci had described invulnerable armed chariots that could push aside the enemy's forces, allowing the infantry to advance unopposed. Patton wrote, "It is a clear description of a tank written 350 years before the first appearance of the successful TANK."[13]

In 1920 the passage of the National Defense Act reestablished the army's primary combat arms as infantry, artillery, and cavalry. Each branch was to be led by a major general responsible for developing its own doctrine and research and development. The Tank Corps was formally abolished, and all tank units and personnel were assigned to the infantry. The position of chief of Tank Corps was eliminated and tankers were now designated as members of "Infantry (Tanks)." Without its independence, the Tank Corps was doomed to shrivel under the neglect of the army's first chief of infantry, Charles Farnsworth. The former head of the Infantry School at Fort Benning, Georgia, Farnsworth had commanded the U.S. Thirty-seventh Division in World War I, receiving the Distinguished Service Medal and the Silver Star.[14] According to Carlo D'Este, Farnsworth "had no fondness for either tanks or the officers who commanded them."[15]

That was the same year Patton reverted to his permanent rank of captain from his wartime appointment as colonel. His quick promotion to major, however, indicates that he was highly thought of, for such promotions had become infrequent in the peacetime army. Eisenhower likewise was demoted and then promoted to major. Patton now faced an important inflection point in his career. He could remain in the infantry or request a transfer back to the cavalry. The likelihood of advancement in the infantry was slim and probably not increased by Patton's lobbying on behalf of the Tank Corps. In the cavalry Patton knew he would find the warm embrace of old friends and familiar traditions and rituals. He decided to return to the cavalry.

Patton's departing speech to the 304th Brigade, Tank Corps, on September 20, 1920, touched on many of the signature elements of his style of leadership—uniting his men through a common fear of their commander, an affinity for cursing, and his dedication to work as hard as his own soldiers:

> [T]hough you probably think me the meanest man in the world I assure you that you exaggerate. I have a great pride and sincere affection for the brigade and the men and the officers composing it.... When I have cussed out or corrected any of you, men or officers, it has been because according to my lights you were wrong, but I have never remembered it against you. I have never asked any of you to brace more, work more, or fight more, than I have been willing to do myself; with the result that in keeping up with you in France I had to get shot. You have always responded, and consequently wherever the brigade or any part of it has served it has been an example of discipline, courage and efficiency.... I was given the Distinguished Service Medal, but be sure that I realize that it was the brigade and not I who won it.... God bless the 304th Brigade.[16]

While traditionalists in the U.S. Army clung to old dogmas about infantry and cavalry, other powers were embracing the tank. In 1928

Russia purchased two tanks manufactured by the American engineer Walter Christie, one of the world's foremost tank designers. The Russians copied and continued to refine what they called the "Christie-Russki," and they eventually developed the powerful T-34 tank, arguably the best tank of World War II. The Soviet commander Mikhail Tukhachevsky developed a theory of "deep operations," according to which combined arms strike deep behind enemy lines to destroy the enemy's rear and supply bases. Tukhachevsky was executed in Stalin's purge of his military in 1937, but his strategy had essentially been adopted by the Red Army.

In Germany, Heinz Guderian wrote many papers on mechanized warfare. In 1937 he published an important book on the subject, *Achtung-Panzer!*, outlining the theories of tank war that became the basis for the German *Panzer* forces and *Blitzkrieg* warfare in World War II. Guderian argued, as did Patton and Eisenhower, that tanks should play a primary role and not be subordinated to infantry divisions.

The U.S. Army, meanwhile, neglected airpower and armor, two military developments that were about to shock the world. The American military attaché in Berlin reported on German developments, as did another American army officer, Major Albert C. Wedemeyer, who had befriended Guderian and Erwin Rommel while attending a war college in Berlin. Patton absorbed the English translations of the writings of Guderian, Rommel, and Walter Warlimont prepared by U.S. Army intelligence. He also scoured the writings of the British apostles of the new form of warfare, men like Liddell Hart and J. F. C. Fuller, as well as a little known French colonel, Charles de Gaulle.

Patton remained a believer in the value of armor, but he also clung to the doomed orthodoxy regarding the cavalry. In a lecture on "Modern Cavalry" delivered at the Marine Corps School at Quantico in 1931, Patton closed with a dramatic (and incorrect) prediction:, "[L]et me say that the greatest ill-luck I can wish those who think the cavalry is dead, is to be against us in the next war. They will be corpses, not we."[17] In a lecture at Fort Myer in 1933, he articulated the many virtues of mechanized forces, both armored vehicles and tanks. In his conclusion however, he undercut much of what he had just said by outlining the new weapons' vulnerabilities and by restating the perpetual need for a cavalry.

Patton's cavalry did take part in one violent confrontation that was a painful episode in the history of the United States military. In 1932, veterans of the world war gathered in Washington, D.C., seeking an immediate payment of the bonuses that were due in 1945. Many of the men had been unemployed since the onset of the Great Depression and desperately needed the money. Eisenhower and Patton were sympathetic to the plight of the marchers but also suspicious that they were being exploited by communists seeking to promote a revolution. Douglas MacArthur viewed the ragtag "Bonus Army" as a communist rabble. On July 28 at 4:45 p.m., the veterans were dispersed by advancing cavalry, including Patton, and troops commanded by MacArthur. Faced with soldiers using fixed bayonets and a primitive form of riot gas, the veterans fled across the Anacostia River, where a shantytown had been erected. President Hoover ordered the assault halted, but MacArthur flagrantly ignored him. He chased the men across the bridge and soon the encampment on the other side of the river was engulfed in flames. Eisenhower, who was MacArthur's aide at the time, was thoroughly disgusted by the action and by MacArthur's role in it. He had strongly advised his commander against taking any public role in the advance against the Bonus Army. Despite his sympathy for the veterans, Patton clearly relished the excitement of the engagement. "In my opinion, the majority were poor, ignorant men, without hope and without really evil intent, but there were several thousand bad men among them and many weak sisters joined them."[18]

One of the Bonus Marchers was Joe Angelo, the orderly who had saved Patton's life at Cheppy. Like Patton, Angelo had received the

Distinguished Service Cross for his heroism. The day after the veterans' violent eviction, Angelo sought a meeting with Patton, which Patton refused. Angelo had become something of a leader of the movement, and Patton feared the press attention that a reunion would invite. Even without the meeting, one newspaper headline read, "Major Ousts Vet Who Saved Life; Bonus Seeker Flees before Officer He Rescued on Battlefield."[19] Patton sought to defend his refusal to meet with Angelo. Speaking to a small group of officers, Patton said, "Since the war my mother and I have more than supported him. We have given him money. We have set him up in business several times. Can you imagine the headlines if the papers got wind of our meeting here this morning!"[20] The Patton family later visited Angelo at Walter Reed Hospital. Beatrice had insisted that her children meet the man who had saved their father's life in World War I.

In typical Patton fashion, he sought to learn from the episode and prepared a paper titled "Federal Troops in Domestic Disturbances." The paper reveals Patton's extensive knowledge of military history—he cites numerous examples of domestic insurrections, such as the Whiskey Rebellion, the unrest associated with the Gracchi, the French Revolution, and the Bolshevik Revolution. The practical lessons he draws include:

> Before firing at a mob warn them of your intention, and tell innocent people to "beat it".... Designate in advance certain sharpshooters to kill individual rioters who fire on or throw missiles at your men. Have even this firing done only on your orders, or that of a commissioned officer.... Should some orator start haranguing the crowd and inciting them to violence grab him even if it brings on a local fight. Small fights are better than big ones.[21]

In the spring of 1935, Patton received orders to return to Hawaii. There he focused his energies on identifying the islands' vulnerability to attack, a growing concern in light of Japan's aggression in Manchuria and China. In another paper, Patton reached "the inescapable assumption that complete surprise offers the greatest opportunity for the successful capture of these islands. It is reliably reported that during the last four years three or more Japanese divisions were embarked, moved to the coast of Asia and disembarked without any military attaché, consular agent, foreign press correspondent or any other foreigner living in Japan being aware of the fact until the troops were in action in Asia." He also noted that an approaching Japanese fleet could depart from islands that were merely seven days' sailing away, and if they moved against Hawaii they would be "streaming over the loneliest sea lanes in the world. Who can say that an expeditionary force is not in these islands now?"[22]

For Patton the interwar period was also a time of personal and emotional crisis, fueled by his fear of aging, his discouragement over the lack of promotion, and the nagging doubt that "his war" would come and allow him to realize his destiny. He began to drink, sought out the company of younger people, and became susceptible to the flirtatious approaches of other women. It was a textbook "midlife crisis," exacerbated by Patton's already emotional and erratic nature. He would occasionally sink into a deep depression that would both trouble and test his family, particularly his wife, Beatrice. More than anyone, Beatrice was Patton's anchor, but even she became exasperated with her husband's prolonged black moods.

The stress would have wrecked most other marriages. Indeed, by 1940 it seems to have resulted in an estrangement between the pair after thirty years of marriage. In his letters to his wife, Patton vacillates between self-pity and sincere apology. He was taking flying lessons, and on one occasion his plane's motor shut down after take-off.

Describing the incident to Beatrice, he wrote, "You almost got your wish that I die soon." But around the same time, he wrote, "I hope some day you may forgive me but I will be damned if I see why you should. I love you anyhow." In another letter he asked for his wife's forgiveness, telling her, "You are the only person I have ever loved."[23]

The battle between horse and machine continued throughout the 1930s. In 1940 the Third Army conducted war games in Louisiana between a cavalry division led by Patton's friend Kenyon Joyce and a provisional division of mechanized and tank forces. Before the maneuvers Patton obtained some inside information on the exercise from the chief of staff of the Third Army, which he shared with Joyce in a letter that concluded, "All good wishes for the success of the horse cavalry."[24] The mechanized forces thoroughly trounced the horse cavalry. Patton acted as an umpire in the maneuvers, which provided him with great insight how mechanized units operated and what their potential was on the battlefield.

Inspired and emboldened by the results, a cabal of officers, including Patton and Adna R. Chaffee Jr., held a clandestine meeting in the basement of a nearby high school. They compiled a list of recommendations—the chief of which was the creation of an independent tank force—that ended up on the desk of the army chief of staff, George C. Marshall. Despite angry protests from the infantry and the cavalry, Marshall acted swiftly to create the Armored Force, and he appointed Chaffee its first commander.[25] It was the last nail in the coffin of the cavalry.

Chaffee had been both a friend and rival of Patton. Unlike Patton, Chaffee had been a vocal proponent of armored forces during the interwar period and became the leading American advocate for tanks. As early as 1927 he predicted that the next war would be dominated by mechanized forces. In 1940, Chaffee told Patton that he had put him on his preferred list as a commander for an armored brigade. He concluded by saying, "I shall always be happy to know that you are around close in any capacity when there is fighting to be done." Patton read in the newspaper soon thereafter that he had received command of the Second Armored Brigade.

Patton deserved the appointment notwithstanding his waffling on the role of armor and his defense of the cavalry. It was General Marshall, however, who had noticed Patton and rescued his career from the cavalry. Patton's biographer Ladislas Farago remarks on Marshall's importance for Patton:

> It was the forceful intervention of something akin to fate which skyrocketed Marshall to a position of dominant influence in the Army and simultaneously as its direct result, saved Patton for his great future service. It is probably no exaggeration to say that without Marshall's phenomenal and rapid rise after years of neglect and ostracism, Patton would have vanished though some trap door in the oblivion of a retired colonel.[26]

For two decades Patton's military career had been marked by frustration and disappointment. It had taken him fourteen years to be promoted from major to lieutenant colonel. He had invested those years in the wrong branch of the service, the cavalry. While he was held in high regard by those who had worked with him, even his supporters winced at some of his emotional displays and his eccentricities. Some saw him as a wealthy socialite who flaunted his money and blatantly curried favor with superiors. He had sorely tested his wife's patience with his personal behavior and emotional outbursts. But as the clouds of war gathered, Patton refocused his energy and attention on the newly formed armored division. In November Patton turned fifty-five years old, but his destiny still lay ahead.

A man of enormous personal bravery, Patton had summoned the courage to face death during the Punitive Expedition and in the Meuse-Argonne Offensive. During World War II, he would insist on leading his men from the front, heedless of the danger of enemy artillery and aircraft. But like his friend Eisenhower, Patton backed down from his advocacy of the tank in the face of threats to his military career. Adna Chaffee assumed the role of visionary champion of the tank, while Patton enjoyed a comfortable and secure existence in the cavalry. It is arguable that Patton's only retreat was an example of admirable (if uncharacteristic) discretion. He preserved his ability to lead troops to victory in World War II. In any case, having forfeited to Chaffee the sobriquet "Father of the Armored Force," Patton ferociously applied everything he had learned in the cavalry to the new, lethal form of warfare.

CHAPTER EIGHT

TEACHING COURAGE

THE SPEECH
WAR GAMES
DESERT TRAINING CENTER
OPERATION TORCH

*"Why, by God, I actually pity those poor sons-of-bitches
we're going up against. By God, I do!"*

—PATTON

In April 1941 Patton, who had been acting commander of the Second Armored Division for six months, was given permanent command and promoted to major general. His most important priority was training men for war. One of his first acts as commander had been to build an amphitheater in the wooded hills of Fort Benning that could accommodate the entire division. It was soon known as the "Patton Bowl." The earliest versions of his soon-to-be-famous "blood and guts" speeches were delivered there. As one soldier recalled:

> I am positive the Patton image was born on the first day he spoke in that bowl. Following an old cavalry credo to the effect you should always "Hit 'em where they ain't," he said

to us: "You have to grab 'em by the [censored] and kick 'em in the [censored]...." At the end of the speech he said, "I am taking this division into Berlin and when I do, I want every one of your tracks to be carrying the stench of German blood and guts."[1]

But it was not just a speech, it was a performance. Patton was not blessed with a deep, booming voice. His voice was actually rather high, certainly not the gravelly bass of George C. Scott in the Hollywood movie *Patton*. But he was a master of the dramatic pause, lowering his voice to great effect, forcing the audience to listen carefully, before bellowing out a line of profanity. With the skill of a method actor, Patton would also strive to achieve an intimidating mien—his "war face"—that would communicate his intensity to his audience.

Many elements of the speech were recycled over and over. Some lines became classic.

* Men this stuff that some sources sling around about America wanting out of this war, not wanting to fight, is a crock of bullshit. Americans love to fight. All real Americans love the sting and clash of battle.
* Americans love a winner. Americans will not tolerate a loser. Americans despise cowards. Americans play to win all of the time. I wouldn't give a hoot in hell for a man who lost and laughed. That's why Americans have never lost and will never lose a war; for the very idea of losing is hateful to an American.
* Death must not be feared. Death, in time, comes to all men. Yes, every man is scared in his first battle. If he says he's not, he's a liar. Some men are cowards but they fight the same as the brave men or they get the hell slammed out of them watching other men fight who are

just as scared as they are. The real hero is the man who fights even though he is scared.... Remember that the enemy is just as frightened as you are, and probably more so.

* A man must be alert at all times if he expects to stay alive. If you're not alert, some time a German son of a bitch is going to sneak up behind you and beat you to death with a sockful of shit!

* An Army is a team. It lives, sleeps, eats, and fights as a team. This individual heroic stuff is pure horseshit. The bilious bastards who write that kind of stuff for the *Saturday Evening Post* don't know any more about real fighting under fire than they know about f***ing!

* We have the finest food, the finest equipment, the best spirit, and the best men in the world. Why, by God, I actually pity those poor sons of bitches we're going up against. By God, I do!

* I don't want to hear of any soldier under my command being captured unless he has been hit. Even if you are hit, you can still fight back.

* All of the real heroes are not storybook combat fighters, either. Every single man in this Army plays a vital role.... Don't ever think that your job is unimportant. Every man has a job to do and he must do it. Every man is a vital link in the great chain.

* Some day I want to see the Germans raise up on their piss-soaked hind legs and howl, "Jesus Christ, it's that goddamned Third Army again and that son of a bitch Patton."

* Sure we want to go home. We want this war over with. The quickest way to get it over with is to go get the bastards who started it. The quicker they are whipped,

the quicker we can go home. The shortest way home is through Berlin and Tokyo. And when we get to Berlin, I am personally going to shoot that paper hanging son of a bitch Hitler, just like I'd shoot a snake!

★ My men don't dig foxholes. I don't want them to. Foxholes only slow up an offensive. Keep moving. And don't give the enemy time to dig one either.[2]

★ We're not just going to shoot the sons of bitches, we're going to rip out their living goddamned guts and use them to grease the treads of our tanks. We're going to murder those lousy Hun bastards by the bushel-f***ing-basket.

★ I don't want to get any messages saying, "I am holding my position." We are not holding a goddamned thing. Let the Germans do that. We are advancing constantly and we are not interested in holding onto anything except the enemy's balls!

★ There is one great thing you men will be able to say when you go home.... Thirty years from now, when you are sitting around the fireside with your grandson on your knee and he asks what you did in the great World War II, you won't have to say, "I shoveled shit in Louisiana."

The vivid and profane inspirational speeches garnered much attention and some detractors, but Patton also gave countless speeches intended to educate his officers and troops on the topics of strategy, tactics, discipline, and how to conduct the new deadly form of armored warfare:

★ You men and officers are, in my opinion, magnificently disciplined.... You cannot be disciplined in great things and undisciplined in small things.... Brave, undisciplined men have no chance against the discipline and valor of other men.

★ An armored division is the most powerful organization ever devised by the mind of men.... An armored division is that element of the team which carries out the running plays. We straight-arm, and go around, and dodge, and go around....

★ People must try to use their imagination and when orders fail to come, must act on their own best judgment. A very safe rule to follow is that in case of doubt, push on just a little further and then keep on pushing....

★ There is still a tendency in each separate unit ... to be a one-handed puncher. By that I mean that the rifleman wants to shoot, the tanker wants to charge, the artilleryman to fire.... That is not the way to win battles. If the band played a piece first with the piccolo, then with the brass horn, then with the clarinet, and then with the trumpet, there would be a hell of a lot of noise but no music.

Patton's speeches typically included humor, almost always profane and often self-deprecatory:

★ I do not know of a better way to die than to be facing the enemy. I pray that I will fall forward when I am shot. That way I can keep firing my pistols! I was shot in the behind in World War I! I do not want to be hit there again. I got a medal for charging at the enemy, but I have had to spend a lot of time explaining how I got shot in the behind!

★ Every man is expendable—especially me.[3]

Patton's communication was not limited to his speeches; he also projected strength in his demeanor and in his dress. He sought to present the striking image of a leader, an image that demanded attention and inspired his troops by its swagger. In 1941, on the day the men of the Second Armored Division completed their orientation at Fort Benning, Patton appeared wearing a new uniform, which, characteristically, he had designed himself. It was a two-piece dark green corduroy outfit. The jacket was waist length with brass buttons up the right side in the style of an old Confederate officer's uniform. The trouser legs were skinny and shoved into his black, laced-up field boots. His head was encased in a tight-fitting leather helmet with goggles. A heavy ivory-handled revolver rested in a shoulder holster draped under his left arm. The admiring troops immediately dubbed him the Green Hornet.[4]

One of Patton's tank commanders, Harry Semmes, described a later incarnation of the Patton uniform:

> He always dressed immaculately and expensively. His combination riding breeches and jodhpurs, with a specially made English combat boot, were distinctive. His famous glistening helmet liner was the result of literally dozens of coats of varnish by his ordnance personnel. Around this shining halo were the insignias of all his former commands, like a garish chaplet. When he traveled he carried an arsenal of guns and extensive wardrobe in several traveling bags....[5]

In 1941, as the American army prepared for the possibility of war, Chief of Staff George C. Marshall ordered that large training maneuvers be conducted in Tennessee, Louisiana, and the Carolinas in order to assess and instruct the inexperienced military. "I want the mistakes [made] down in Louisiana, not over in Europe, and the only way to do this thing is to try it out, and if it doesn't work, find out what we need to make it work," said Marshall. They were the largest military exercises the United States had ever conducted. War seemed increasingly certain. It was just a matter of how soon. At the end of 1940 the army had 620,000 men; only six months later, with the institution of the draft, that number had more than doubled to 1.4 million.[6]

In mid-June Patton took his division to Camp Forrest, Tennessee, where reporters dubbed it "America's answer to the Panzer division." Patton's own nickname for the unit was "Hell on Wheels," and he described it as "the most powerful striking force the human mind has ever developed." In the first exercise, the infantry was able to blunt the advance of Patton's tanks. It was a setback for the armored division, which delivered an unimpressive performance, and Patton was criticized for failing to coordinate his unit's operation. In the next game, Patton redeemed himself with slashing cavalry-like tactics, reconnoitering during the day and then attacking at night. By nine a.m. the following day, Patton's men had captured the opposing team's command post and taken the "enemy" general and his staff prisoner. Just two hours later, well in advance of the scheduled end of the game, the umpires declared the second exercise over. In the next war game, Patton's division undertook a Blitzkrieg-like strike, slicing through the enemy's defenses and forcing him to capitulate in just nine hours. In the last exercise, Patton's force enveloped the opposing army, cutting its lines of communication and disrupting its rear area. When they captured the town of Tullahoma, the objective of the game, the exercise concluded, once again hours ahead of schedule.

Despite his success in the Tennessee war games, Patton was criticized by the umpires for failing to use his armored division to launch concentrated attacks. Patton responded in writing that the criticism was actually the "greatest compliment possible." Mass armor attacks were a legacy of World War I, when tanks were invulnerable. He also refuted the notion that the role of an armored division was to attack and destroy the enemy. Patton instead employed his armor as mechanized cavalry troops to get behind an enemy and disrupt his supply lines, thereby making him vulnerable to destruction by infantry and artillery units.[7]

Patton also came under attack by the umpires for leaving his command post. It was a criticism that Patton predictably rejected. "Were the commanding general of an armored division to sit anywhere with information three hours old, his units might well be from 15 to 25 miles from the point indicated on the map." Patton also pointed out that a division commander had to be in a position to see how well the troops carried out what they had been trained to do. "He cannot get this knowledge at a desk."[8] In any event, as he had demonstrated in World War I when he defied his superior's orders to remain at the command post, Patton's nature demanded that he be closer to the fighting troops.

The Louisiana maneuvers (which spilled over into eastern Texas) took place in August and September. About four hundred thousand soldiers took part, including the I Armored Corps. Patton's reputation was enhanced by his division's performance, with the umpires and observers noting that Patton's unit had ridden roughshod over the opponent. Patton wrote a letter to Pershing noting that in each of the ten maneuver attacks his division had achieved its objective. "I am quite sure this is a unique record both as to success and as to number of operations," Patton boasted.[9]

Carlo D'Este describes Patton's leadership in the Louisiana exercise:

> Patton had driven his men with his usual combination of enthusiasm and whip-cracking, and personal example. When his tanks ran out of gas, the division paid in cash

(possibly Patton's) to have them refueled at local filling stations. Patton's journey actually took his division outside the designated maneuver area, resulting in howls of outrage that he was playing by his own rules. Patton merely grinned and retorted that he was unaware of any rules in war. Winning war was all that mattered, and he did not give a damn what it took so long as the enemy was defeated.[10]

The Carolina maneuvers took place in November. Patton would face off against Hugh Drum, his former commander in Hawaii. On the first day of the final phase of the exercise, Drum was captured at a roadblock by Patton's forces. While being taken to the rear, presumably for a humiliating encounter with Patton, Drum was ordered to be released by General McNair, the director of the exercise. Possibly to spare Drum further humiliation, McNair claimed that Drum would not have been successfully taken through his own lines. His release also conveniently allowed the exercise to continue. The episode, however, almost certainly shortened Drum's military career, and he retired in obscurity a couple of years later. The Carolina maneuvers concluded on December 1. Six days later, on a quiet Sunday morning in Honolulu, the Japanese bombed Pearl Harbor.

Shortly after the conclusion of the exercises, the army began making plans to join their British allies in their desert campaign in North Africa. But first the Americans would need training in desert warfare, which required both a desert training center and a commander. Fresh from his impressive performance in the army's war maneuvers, Patton was selected on January 31, 1942, by Lieutenant General Lesley J. McNair to quickly establish the army's desert training facilities. Patton selected an area of southern California just two hours east of his hometown of San Gabriel. The training area covered a vast and rugged wasteland stretching from Indio, California (near Palm Springs) to Aguila, Arizona, and a million soldiers would train there. Many recruits, upon learning they would be heading to California, envisioned beautiful beaches and Hollywood glamour. They were dropped into a barren desert, not at the beach, and were greeted by scorpions instead of starlets. The twenty thousand-square-mile training ground was a monotony of desert and mountain landscapes, populated with cactus, scrub brush, mesquite, rattlesnakes, and jackrabbits. It was dubbed "Little Libya," but most of the soldiers called it simply "the place that God forgot."

Patton issued orders that all soldiers be able to run a mile in ten minutes while wearing their full field packs and carrying their rifles. He permitted his men only one canteen of water per day and minimal food. He wanted his men to acclimate to the punishing desert heat, which could soar to 130 degrees in the shade in the summer but drop below freezing at night in the winter.

Patton presented his thoughts on training in a paper titled "Notes on Tactics and Techniques of Desert Warfare":

* ⋆ "There is a regrettable and widespread belief among civilians and in the Army that we will win this war through materiel. In my opinion we will only win this war through blood, sacrifice, and high courage."[11]
* ⋆ "You win war with guts not machines."[12]
* ⋆ "In order to get willing fighters we must develop the highest possible Esprit de Corps. Therefore, the removal of distinctive badges and insignia from the uniform is highly detrimental. To die willingly, as many of us must, we must have tremendous pride not only in our nation and in ourselves but in the unit in which we serve.... The Romans had distinctive standards; so had the Gauls."[13]
* ⋆ " Formation and materiel are of very secondary importance compared to discipline, the ability to shoot rapidly

and accurately with the proper weapon at the proper
target, and the irresistible desire to close with the enemy
with the purpose of killing and destroying him."[14]

Eisenhower wrote to Patton from Washington lamenting that he
was stuck at a desk job and predicting that Patton would be the "Black
Jack" Pershing of the coming war. Patton responded that he would
welcome Eisenhower as his assistant or "even the other way around."[15]

One of Patton's guiding principles of leadership was that troops
should fear their own commander more than the enemy. An incident
at the Desert Training Center, recounted by Carlo D'Este, illustrates
that Patton had achieved this objective:

To ensure that his troops remained alert, Patton frequently
attempted to infiltrate his own heavily guarded base camp.
One night he was prowling outside its perimeter with Lieutenant Williamson, whom he sent forward to see if the
guard knew his instructions. When asked from what direction he expected trouble, the guard pointed directly at
Patton's headquarters in the center of camp and replied
that was where he expected trouble. Patton, who overheard
the conversation, began laughing, and waved off Williamson. "That man understands his mission."[16]

At 10:45 a.m., on July 30, 1942, when he was in his office in Indio,
Patton received the call that was to bring him a step closer to fulfilling
his destiny. "General, I am calling you by the order of General Marshall. He wants to see you here in Washington as soon as you can leave
the Center." Patton was told to prepare for a long absence from Indio;
in fact, he might never return to the Desert Training Center. The call
launched Patton on his career as America's most famous combat general. As Ladislas Farago writes:

It was the hottest day of the year in the desert, the ther-
mometer hitting 120 degrees. Patton was alone in his big
office, its stillness on this routine morning, when nothing
extraordinary was expected to happen, mellowed by the
monotonous purring of the air conditioner. With his acute
sense of destiny, he recognized immediately that that call
was the turning point in his life…. When he hung up, and
before he did anything else, he went through the ritual he
invariably performed upon receipt of momentous messages
which signaled upward turns in his fortune. George Patton
went down on his knees and prayed.[17]

Patton had never doubted that his summons to greatness in battle
would come sooner or later. He had always believed his fortunes were
predetermined by God, while recognizing that at times he tested not
only his commanders' patience but also his Creator's.

When Patton arrived in Washington, D.C., he was taken directly
to General Marshall. "Patton," Marshall said, "I have just returned
from London with what we must regard as the second-best solution
we can expect under the circumstances to take the offensive against
the Axis this year." Marshall's original proposal had been to launch a
limited-objective attack into Europe in 1942, establishing a bridgehead
in Brest or Cherbourg to relieve pressure on the Russians in the east.
His plan was rejected by the British generals. Instead, an operation
was being planned for a joint British and American invasion of French
North Africa. Churchill gave the secret invasion plan the code name
"Torch." The attack was to be conducted by October 30, 1942—just
three months away.

Marshall held Patton in high regard and seemed to be fond of him
despite his mercurial behavior and occasional temper tantrums.
Marshall's official biographer speculates on what drove Marshall's
selection of Patton to lead Torch:

Perhaps it was a sign of some inner regret in Marshall that he would never have a chance to prove himself in conflict that he prized the eccentrics like Patton and Wingate who were difficult to live with but who exulted in the fray. Or it may have been the temper and the fury of his own nature, rigidly disciplined and long pent up, responding sympathetically to natures that were never curbed. Whatever his reason, he called Patton to fighting command and saw that he had his chance.[18]

Patton thanked the Lord for his selection, but as Farago notes, "it was General Marshall, the Chief of Staff, who decided to give the American command in 'Torch' to that 's.o.b. nobody wanted'—George Patton."[19]

In their meeting, Marshall warned Patton, "You must understand that the job will have to be done with the troops and equipment the planning staff will allot you." Patton nodded his assent, but when he was taken to the War College and presented with the rudimentary plans for the invasion, he bluntly informed Marshall's deputy that the force was inadequate. "I need a great many more men and a lot more ships to do the job." When Marshall was informed of Patton's reaction, the chief of staff quietly responded, "Order him back to Indio."[20]

Patton was returned to the Desert Training Center as fast as he had come to Washington. He stewed for two days before calling Marshall, only to be told that Marshall was busy and could not take his call. This rebuff only made Patton more anxious, and he called several more times without reaching Marshall. Finally an exasperated Patton resignedly gave his message to Marshall's deputy, General Joseph T. McNarney. "Hello, Joe, I did a lot of thinking in the meantime, and I came to the conclusion that maybe I could do the job after all with the forces your stupid staff is willing to give me." McNarney dutifully relayed the conversation to Marshall who, breaking into a smile, said,

"Order him back to the War College. You see, McNarney, that's the way you handle Patton."[21]

As the date for his departure for North Africa drew near, Patton called on his aging mentor General John J. Pershing at Walter Reed Hospital. The old general, now eighty-two, at first did not recognize Patton, but his mind quickly cleared as soon as Patton began to speak. Patton thanked Pershing for having given him his start and taking him to Mexico on the Punitive Expedition in search of Pancho Villa and his militia. Pershing replied, "I can always pick a fighting man and God knows there are few of them. I am happy they are sending you to the front at once. I like generals who are so bold that they are dangerous. I hope they give you a free hand." Before Patton left, he knelt down on one knee, kissed Pershing's hand, and asked for his blessing. As he squeezed Patton's hand, Pershing said, "Good-bye, Georgie, God bless and keep you and give you victory." Patton then stood up, saluted and left. It occurred to him that this was probably the last time he would see Pershing, and also that Pershing could still outlive him. As it turned out, both predictions were true. Patton never saw Pershing again, and Pershing survived to 1948, when he succumbed to congestive heart failure and coronary artery disease, having outlived Patton by two and a half years.[22]

Shortly before setting sail for North Africa, Patton had dinner with his in-laws. After the meal, the stress of the weeks of preparations and the burden of command broke through Patton's typical bluster and bravado. He became "almost hysterical," his brother-in-law, Fred Ayer Jr., recalled, relating a recurring nightmarish vision he had. "It's god awful. It's terrible, that's what it is. I can see it in a vision. It comes to me at night. I am standing there knee-deep in the water and all around as far as the eye can see are dead men, floating like a school of dynamited fish. And they're all floating face up with their eyes wide open and their skins a ghastly white. And they're all looking at me as they float by and saying, 'Patton, you bastard, it's your fault. You did this to me. You killed me.' I can't stand it, I tell you. By God, I won't go. I won't go." "But of course, he did go," Ayer wrote later.[23]

Patton was bored and restless during the two-week voyage across the Atlantic, since the plans for the invasion had been completed. He exercised by running in place in his quarters and using a rowing machine. He lectured his officers on a simple directive of war: "Use steamroller strategy, that is, make up your mind on a course and direction of action and stick to it. But in tactics do not steamroller. Attack weakness. Hold them by the nose and kick them in the arse."[24]

During the Atlantic crossing Patton, ever the student, read a copy of the Koran, better to understand the Muslim population of North Africa. He described it in his diary as "a good book and interesting."[25] Four days later, on November 6, he wrote:

> In forty hours I shall be in battle, with little information, and on the spur of the moment will have to make most momentous decisions, but I believe that one's spirit enlarges with responsibility and that, with God's help, I shall make them and make them right. It seems that my whole life has been pointed to this moment. When this job is done, I presume I will be pointed to the next step in the ladder of destiny. If I do my full duty, the rest will take care of itself.[26]

In early November, Patton wrote a letter to be read to his troops while still at sea:

> Soldiers: We are to be congratulated because we have been chosen as the units of the United States Army best trained to take part in this great American effort....
>
> When the great day of battle comes, remember your training and remember above all that speed and vigor of attack are the sure roads to success, and you must succeed—

for to retreat is as cowardly as it is fatal. Indeed, once landed, retreat is impossible. Americans do not surrender.[27]

During the first few days and nights after you get ashore, you must work unceasingly, regardless of sleep, regardless of food. A pint of sweat will save a gallon of blood.

The eyes of the world are watching us; the heart of America beats for us; God is with us. On our victory depends the freedom or slavery of the human race. We shall surely win.[28]

Operation Torch was organized into three separate amphibious task forces, targeting key ports and airports in French Morocco and Algeria. Patton's Western Task Force was assigned Casablanca,[29] which Patton took on November 11. "A nice birthday present," Patton noted. He was fifty-seven years old. The battle of Casablanca was won with a total of 337 American soldiers and sailors killed, 637 wounded, 122 missing, and 71 captured.[30] "To God be praise," Patton concluded in his diary.[31]

The day before he had written to Eisenhower, his new boss, "I feel that in successfully accomplishing the job you handed me, this force achieved the impossible.... I am forced to believe that either my proverbial luck or more probably the direct intervention of the Lord was responsible."[32] During the fighting Patton had lost his radio and was not able to communicate regularly with Eisenhower, who in the fog of battle had received conflicting reports, including one that said Patton had reembarked under a flag of truce. It was a notion that Eisenhower immediately dismissed—"Unless my opinion of Georgie is 100-percent wrong."[33]

CHAPTER NINE

TASK FORCE BAUM

*"We are headed right for John's place and may
get there before he is moved."*

—Patton's letter to his wife Beatrice, March 23, 1945

O n the night of March 22, 1945, elements of the Third Army crossed the Rhine at the German town of Oppenheim.[1] To their surprise, they were not opposed by enemy forces. Patton, not wanting to compromise his army's success with publicity, telephoned Omar Bradley the following morning and uncharacteristically told him to keep it a secret. "Brad, don't tell anyone, but I'm across." A surprised Bradley responded, "Well, I'll be damned. You mean across the Rhine?" "Sure am," Patton replied, "I sneaked a division over last night. But there are so few Krauts around there they don't know it yet. So don't make any announcement—we'll keep it a secret until we see how it goes." By that evening, the Germans had discovered Patton's forces, and perhaps more important, Patton's British rival, Field Marshall Bernard Montgomery, was preparing to cross the Rhine as well. So Patton called Bradley again. "Brad, for God's sake tell the world we're across.... I want the world to know Third Army made it before Monty starts across," he shouted.[2]

The following day Patton arrived at the pontoon bridge his engineers had constructed over the Rhine. He made his way halfway across the bridge before suddenly halting. "I've been looking forward to this for a long time," Patton said as he unzipped his fly and urinated into the river while an Army photographer recorded the moment for posterity.[3] When he reached the other side of the river, Patton pretended to stumble, imitating William the Conqueror, who famously fell on his face when landing in England but transformed the bad omen into a propitious one by leaping to his feet with a handful of English soil, claiming it portended his complete possession of the country. Patton similarly arose, clutching two handfuls of German earth in his fingers, and exclaimed, "Thus, William the Conqueror!"[4] That evening Patton sent a communiqué to General Eisenhower: "Dear SHAEF [Supreme Headquarters Allied Expeditionary Force], I have just pissed into the Rhine River. For God's sake, send some gasoline."[5]

On March 23, 1945, Eisenhower wrote a warm letter to Patton:

> I have frequently had occasion to state, publicly, my appreciation of the great accomplishments of this Allied force during the past nine months. The purpose of this note is to express to you personally my deep appreciation of the splendid way in which you have conducted Third Army operations from the moment it entered battle last August 1. You have made your Army a fighting force that is not excelled in effectiveness by any other of equal size in the world, and I am very proud of the fact that you, as one of the fighting commanders who has been with me from the beginning of the African campaign, have performed so brilliantly throughout.

We are now fairly started on that phase of the campaign
which I hope will be the final one. I know that Third Army
will be in at the finish in the same decisive way that it has
performed in all the preliminary battles.[6]

A week before the Rhine crossing, Patton had held a press conference in which he delivered a classic performance, mixing the humor-
ous, provocative, and the profane. He announced that the Third Army
would shortly capture its 230,000th prisoner of war. Having previ-
ously been denied permission to photograph the face of the 200,000th
prisoner (the Geneva Convention required that a prisoner be protected
against acts of "public curiosity"), Patton announced that "this time
we will take a picture of his ass." (A week later their POW capture
would top 300,000.) Patton also requested the help of the press corps
in informing the Germans that four of his armored divisions were
slashing away at them. The publicity was "not for me—God knows
I've got enough—I could go to heaven and St. Peter would recognize
me right away—but it is for the officers and the men." Patton then
complained "that the Marines go to town by reporting the number [of
their men] killed, I always try to fight without getting [our] people
killed."[7]

Patton was a hero—to his men, to his superiors at SHAEF, to the
public, and to the press. In the experience of George Patton this could
only mean one thing—something bad was about to happen. Patton
himself wrote to his wife on March 23, "I am really scared by my good
luck." He was right to be worried. Perhaps the most controversial
episode of Patton's career was about to unfold.

On March 26, Patton ordered one of his subordinate commanders,
Major General Manton S. Eddy, who led XII Corps, to send an expedition across the Main River to the town of Hammelburg. As Patton
explained in his memoir, *War As I Knew It*, "There were two purposes
in this expedition: first, to impress the Germans with the idea that we

were moving due east, whereas we intended to move due north, and second, to release some nine hundred American prisoners of war who were at Hammelburg."[8] What Patton neglected to mention was that securing the release of one of those prisoners was of particular interest to him. As he had written the day before in a letter to his wife, "Hope to send an expedition tomorrow to get John."[9]

"John" was Lieutenant Colonel John K. Waters, Patton's son-in-law. Waters had married the Pattons' daughter Beatrice in 1934. A graduate of the United States Military Academy and a cavalry officer, Waters was captured in Tunisia in February 1943 when German forces attacked Sidi Bouzid. The news that Waters was missing was devastating to the Patton family. Patton wrote to his wife that if it had been his own son, George, who had disappeared, "I could not feel worse." Patton recovered an ammunition clip from a burned out tank at the battle site and send it to Waters's children as a memento of their father in case he never returned.[10] When Patton's wife called her daughter to inform her that her husband was missing, after a short silence she replied, "I am sure Johnny's alive." She was right. Several weeks later they received news that Waters was a prisoner of war in Germany.[11]

Patton and Waters had enjoyed a brief reunion in Tunisia before John's capture. Waters commanded a tank battalion in the First Armored Division, and he told Patton how he had narrowly escaped being wounded when a bullet had passed through his uniform but missed his flesh. Patton was disgusted to learn that he was the first general the men of the First Armored Division had seen during their twenty-four days of combat—a "sad commentary on our idea of leadership," he grumbled.[12] One soldier is reported to have remarked in Tunisia, "Never were so few commanded by so many from so far away."[13]

The Americans' disastrous defeats at Sidi Bouzid and Kasserine Pass were as much failures of leadership as they were of inferior equipment and poor tactics. The after-action report on Kasserine labeled Major General Lloyd Fredendall, the American commander of II Corps, a "son of a bitch" who was unfit for command. The report's author later told Patton that Fredendall was a moral and physical coward. When Eisenhower asked the British general Harold Alexander his opinion of Fredendall, Alexander tersely replied, "I'm sure you must have better men than that." Indeed Eisenhower did. Fredendall was relieved of command and replaced with Patton.[14] Ironically, the unmitigated defeat that led to his son-in-law's capture led to Patton's elevation to command and propelled him toward his historic destiny.

The troubling question for those undertaking the mission, and debated by historians since, was whether the rescue of Waters was merely incidental to the Hammelburg mission, or was Patton risking the lives of his men on a dangerous thrust into enemy territory primarily to rescue his son-in-law—"our blood, his guts," as critics have put it. Patton's diary makes no mention of the raid's diversionary purpose. Patton had risked his career before, but this time the potential for disaster was higher than ever.

Patton's two subordinates immediately protested the idea of a raid on Hammelburg. Major General William M. Hoge, commander of the Fourth Armored Division, and XII Corps' Major General Eddy, both thought the mission was "ill-timed, poorly conceived, and under-manned—ill-timed in that it came following several days of hard fighting by the same group of men who had just been given the orders to liberate the camp."[15] After crossing the Rhine on March 24, the men had arrived at the Main two days later after continuous fighting and going without sleep for days.

The mission was to be conducted by units from the famed Fourth Armored Division, one of only two divisions in the European theater to have been awarded a Presidential Unit Citation. The man selected to plan the mission was thirty-year-old Lieutenant Colonel Creighton Abrams, the future commander of U.S. forces in Vietnam and army chief of staff. Abrams initially selected his old friend Lieutenant Colonel Harold Cohen to lead the raid. Cohen, however, was suffering from a severe case of hemorrhoids. Patton, who insisted on personally inspecting Cohen's inflammation, declared, "That is some sorry ass!" and removed him from the assignment.[16]

Cohen's replacement was a twenty-four-year-old captain, Abraham "Abe" Baum, a husky tanker from the Bronx. Patton told the young captain, "Listen, Abe, you pull this off and I'll see to it that you get the Congressional Medal of Honor." Baum had already distinguished himself in battle, earning two Bronze and two Silver Stars. But he was Jewish, and the raid deep into Nazi territory entailed special personal risk.[17] The Jewish New Yorker lent his name to the group undertaking the mission, which became known as "Task Force Baum."

One of Patton's most trusted aides, Major Alexander Stiller, who had served with Patton as a tanker in World War I, accompanied Task Force Baum. He had one particular qualification for the mission that was presumably of interest to Patton—he knew John Waters and could readily identify him. Patton asked Stiller, who had not slept in forty-eight hours, whether he would like to accompany the task force. Stiller understandably thought this to be an order—"a request by a general is an order." When Stiller assented, Patton instructed him to report to Eddy, who in turn told him to report to Hoge.

Hoge informed Stiller of the composition of the task force that Abrams and Cohen had assembled—ten medium tanks, six light tanks, twenty-seven half-tracks, seven jeeps, three motorized assault guns, and a cargo carrier called a weasel. Hoge then asked Stiller what he thought of it. Stiller said he thought the force was too small for the mission. He anticipated that the force would be dropping off soldiers to guard bridges that they would need to cross on the return journey. The task force was strong enough to get to Hammelburg, Stiller said, but he did not think it was strong enough to return. Hoge's response had to unsettle Stiller. He said he did not expect the task force to get back. Hoge explained he was opposed to sending the task force at all.[18]

Stiller then reported to Baum, who was obviously suspicious of Stiller's presence on the task force. A major, Stiller outranked Baum, but Baum was leading the group. Stiller sought to assure Baum that he was merely along "for the thrills and laughs." Baum invited Stiller to ride in his command jeep. Once the task force rolled toward its destination, Baum questioned Stiller again about his presence on the mission, his curiosity as to why the aide to a famous general would accompany a combat mission heading forty miles behind enemy lines obviously not satisfied. "It's important to General Patton," replied Stiller, who then explained that one of the prisoners in the camp was Lieutenant Colonel Waters.

"Who's Colonel Waters?" asked Baum.

"He's Patton's son-in-law," answered Stiller. "Didn't you know that?"

Baum was floored. He was leading three hundred men on an incredibly dangerous mission to save one man? He briefly considered aborting the mission before collecting himself and committing himself again to carrying out his orders.[19]

Martin Blumenson describes the initial stages of the mission:

> Task Force Baum slipped out of the Aschaffenburg area under the cover of early morning darkness and in the confusion of an attack launched to the north. Hammelburg was only 40 miles away, and the vehicles traveled uneventfully for 20 miles. At Lohr, the task force met a small German tank unit moving westward. Baum's men destroyed 12 German tanks and rushed on. A few miles beyond, they knocked out an antiaircraft train. At Gemunden, they shot up a dozen locomotives in the railroad yard. There too was a bridge defended and wired for demolition, and the small

German unit guarding it blew up the structure in Baum's face.[20]

The destruction of the bridge required that the task force improvise their plans. Baum detoured his men six miles north to Burgsinn, an old walled city with a narrow city gate and narrow streets. If the Germans had been alert, they could easily have obstructed the entrance to the town or its streets, but Task Force Baum continued unimpeded. On the way to the next town, Grafendorf, the task force liberated an estimated seven hundred conscripted Russian laborers who were constructing a bridge guarded by German soldiers. The Germans surrendered, and the Russians mobbed Baum's jeep, shouting, "Amerikanski! Amerikanski!" Now armed with their former captors' rifles, the Russians told Baum they wanted to take the town of Burgsinn, a proposal Baum approved on the condition that they wait until the task force had passed. He also handed over the two hundred German prisoners he and his men had captured.[21]

The thrust toward Hammelburg predictably rang alarm bells in the German area command headquarters. Many of the reports exaggerated the task force's strength to the size of an entire division. A small private plane circling over Baum's position, however, was able accurately to estimate the size and location of the American force, enabling the Germans to prepare their counter-attack.

When Baum came into Hammelburg from the west, by pure coincidence a German assault gun battalion also entered the town, but from the east. The two forces engaged in a two-hour firefight before the Americans overcame the defenders and headed for the prison, where the German commander decided to surrender. Four American prisoners, one of whom was Waters, volunteered to communicate the surrender of the prison to the task force. While the group walked out of the prison under a white flag of truce, a German guard shot and severely wounded Waters. At the same time, some of Baum's tanks knocked down part of the camp's barbed wire enclosure, and thousands of joyful, liberated prisoners streamed out, surrounding the task force. The camp held about five thousand prisoners, fifteen hundred of whom were Americans.[22]

A few hours later Baum loaded as many of the Americans on his tanks and in his personnel carrier as possible. The rest were instructed to wait at the camp to be re-liberated by a larger force that would presumably arrive within days, or to escape into the woods and attempt to make their way back to American lines.

But Hoge's prediction was right. The task force would never make it back. Task Force Baum, surrounded by elements of at least three German divisions, was slowly destroyed in a series of increasingly desperate firefights. The last order Baum shouted to his men was "Fan out…make your way west in groups of twos and threes, and go your own way so you won't be visible. Get as much distance between you and them before they get here. Get going!" With that, Baum himself headed into the woods. As he did he removed his dog tags and threw them into the forest. Baum had heard stories of atrocities being inflicted on Jews in Nazi captivity and wanted to discard the identification stamped with the telltale "H" for Hebrew. Baum and most of his men wound up, for a short time, as prisoners in the camp they had temporarily liberated. The Germans never discovered that he had been the leader of the daring mission to Hammelburg. It was inconceivable to them that the raid that had caused them so much disruption could have been led by a twenty-four-year old captain.[23]

Patton came to Baum's hospital bedside and awarded him the Distinguished Service Cross. "You did one helluva job," Patton said. "I always knew you were one of the best." Baum replied, "You know, sir, it's difficult for me to believe that you would have sent us on that mission just to rescue one man."

"That's right, Abe, I wouldn't," said Patton. He then promised to return Baum to the Fourth Armored Division, as he had requested. When Patton left, one of the general's aides told Baum that the task force had been classified top secret, and that he was to use discretion when discussing it. To Baum, this meant that he and his men were being "screwed again," with no public recognition for their heroism and sacrifice. Baum also suspected that he was not recommended for a Medal of Honor to avoid closer scrutiny of the raid, which Patton and the army now sought to cover up by classifying it.[24]

Patton's claims that he had no idea that John Waters was being held in the prison camp at Hammelburg seem to be undercut by his own letters to his wife and comments made by his aides. On March 27 Patton wrote to Beatrice, "Last night I sent an armored column to a place 40 miles east of Frankfurt where John and some 900 prisoners are said to be. I have been nervous as a cat all day as every one but me thought it too great a risk. I hope it works. Al Stiller went along. If I lose that column it will probably be a new incident, but I won't lose it."[25] Two days later Patton wrote his brother-in-law, Frederick Ayer, "Some days ago I heard of an American prisoner of war camp...so I sent an armored expedition to get it. So far I have not been able to hear what they did. It is possible that John may be among the prisoners. If so, I will be very delighted to take the place."[26]

When Hoge and Eddy both objected to Patton's orders to carry out the raid, Stiller explained to Hoge that "the 'Old Man' was absolutely determined to free the prisoners at Hammelburg—and also revealed that John Waters, Patton's son-in-law, was one of the prisoners."[27] John Toland writes that the head of the U.S. Military Mission to Russia, Major General John Deane, learned that Waters and other American prisoners of war were marched from their camp in Poland to Oflag XIIIB in Hammelburg. This information was transmitted to Eisenhower, who then communicated it to Patton.[28] Prisoners present

Lt. George Patton (fifth from left) with Gen. John J. Pershing (fourth from left) at U.S. field headquarters near Casas Grandes, Mexico, during the Punitive Expedition, 1916.

Col. George S. Patton Jr. in World War I.

Patton watches M3 fight tanks on maneuvers, 1942.

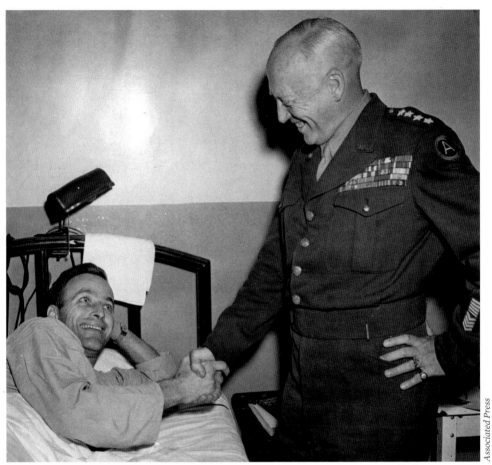

Patton visits his rescued son-in-law, Lt. Col. John Waters, at Walter Reed Hospital, June 1945.

Lipizzaner stallions at the Spanish Riding School, Vienna, 1936.

Patton with Congresswoman Clare Booth Luce, whom he assured that he read the Bible "every goddamned day."

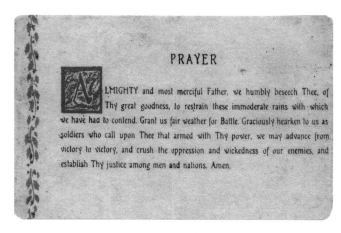

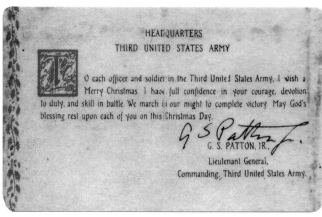

PRAYER

ALMIGHTY and most merciful Father, we humbly beseech Thee, of Thy great goodness, to restrain these immoderate rains with which we have had to contend. Grant us fair weather for Battle. Graciously hearken to us as soldiers who call upon Thee that armed with Thy power, we may advance from victory to victory, and crush the oppression and wickedness of our enemies, and establish Thy justice among men and nations. Amen.

HEADQUARTERS
THIRD UNITED STATES ARMY

To each officer and soldier in the Third United States Army, I wish a Merry Christmas. I have full confidence in your courage, devotion to duty, and skill in battle. We march in our might to complete victory. May God's blessing rest upon each of you on this Christmas Day.

G. S. PATTON, JR.,
Lieutenant General,
Commanding, Third United States Army.

The prayer for good weather and Christmas greeting that Patton had distributed to the 250,000 men of the Third Army, 1944.

Getty Images

"The last enemy that shall be conquered is fear of death." Patton's grave in Hamm, Luxembourg.

"I have fought a good fight. I have finished my course. I have kept the faith." The Patton Memorial Window in the Church of Our Saviour, San Gabriel, California. Patton was baptized and confirmed in this church, which was founded by his grandfather, Benjamin Davis Wilson.

at the camp also reported that the first words of the officer in charge of Task Force Baum as they crashed the gates of the camp were "Where is Colonel Walters?"[29]

Waters had been seriously wounded during Baum's liberation of the camp. His life was saved by a Serbian doctor, a fellow prisoner, who treated him with paper bandages and a kitchen knife. The bullet had struck him "in the left groin but below the peritoneal cavity. The bullet went through the rectum, knocked the end off his coccyx, and came out his left hip."[30] Hammelburg was liberated a second time on April 5 by the Fourteenth Armored Division. Patton sent his personal physician and two cub planes to airlift Waters to Frankfurt. Waters' first question when he finally saw his father-in-law was, "Did you know I was there?" The question perhaps betrays Waters' sense or concern that the raid had been ordered for his personal benefit. Patton replied, "I didn't know but thought you might be there."[31] Waters went on to make a full recovery and return to active duty in 1946. He would later serve as the commandant of cadets at West Point and eventually attain the rank of four-star general.

Did Patton bear sole responsibility for the Hammelburg raid? Did Patton's superior Omar Bradley have any knowledge of the plan and therefore bear any culpability? In a letter to his wife dated April 5, 1945, Patton wrote, "My first thought was to send a combat command, but I was talked out of it by Omar and others...."[32] In his own war memoir, *A Soldier's Story*, Bradley insisted that he knew nothing of the raid beforehand. "Certainly had George consulted me on the mission, I would have forbidden him to stage it." Bradley's failure to rebuke Patton for his purportedly independent action, however, may indicate that Bradley had some foreknowledge and hence responsibility for the raid. Bradley's reason for not disciplining Patton rings false given the punishments exacted for prior and arguably lesser transgressions. "But while I deplored the impetuousness that had driven

Patton, I did not rebuke him," writes Bradley. "Failure itself was George's own worst reprimand."[33]

The war diary of Bradley's aide, Colonel Joe Hansen, seems to contradict Bradley's claim of ignorance. In an entry dated March 28, 1945, Hansen wrote: "When Patton ran off on his mission the other day, Brad told him he would allow it provided Patton did not become involved. He was ordered to withdraw if he did to prevent him from becoming entangled in the wrong direction."[34]

Patton discussed the raid at a press conference on April 13, 1945, at Herzfeld, Germany. He explained that the task force had been sent "for the purpose of misleading the Germans and make them think we were going to Nuremberg but actually [it] went to rescue the 900 American prisoners there, got to its objective. They met the 2d Panzer Division and two other divisions, which showed that our effort to mislead the enemy had its effect, because [had] he [the enemy] put these divisions up north, our efforts there would have been much slower." The same day he wrote to his wife that the reporters were trying to make an incident "out of my attempt to rescue John. How I hate the press."[35] Luckily for Patton the raid at Hammelburg escaped the extraordinary press scrutiny that had attended his earlier embarrassments. He benefitted greatly in this regard by the death of President Franklin Roosevelt, who passed away on April 12, 1945. There seemed to be no appetite for the story in the wake of the president's death and with the rejoicing over the end of the war in Europe. "What the hell! With the President's death you could execute public buggery in the streets and get no farther than the fourth page."[36]

There are two other factors that may have motivated Patton to order the Hammelburg raid. Patton claimed to have feared that American prisoners might be massacred by the retreating Germans "in their last death struggles."[37] This concern proved to be unfounded but was commonly voiced, especially following the Malmedy massacre during the Battle of the Bulge. Patton may also have been

competitively driven by MacArthur's liberation of two prison camps
in the Philippines a month earlier. Blumenson writes that "Patton
was reported to have said that he would make MacArthur look like
a piker."[38]

On April 15, 1945, Eisenhower sent a message to General Marshall
explaining the affair and ultimately defending Patton:

> He sent off a little expedition on a wild goose chase in an
> effort to liberate some American prisoners. The upshot was
> that he got 25 prisoners back and lost a full company of
> medium tanks and a platoon of light tanks. Foolishly, he
> then imposed censorship on the movement, meaning to lift
> it later, which he forgot to do. The story has now been
> released, and I hope the newspapers do not make too much
> of it. One bad though, Patton says accidental, feature of the
> affair was that his own son-in-law was one of the 25
> released. Patton is a problem child, but he is a great fighting
> leader in pursuit and exploitation.[39]

How should Patton be judged for the Hammelburg raid? Was it a
legitimate diversionary feint to draw attention away from the Third
Army's push north? Or was the main purpose actually to free Patton's
son-in-law? Carlo D'Este reserves his harshest criticism of Patton for
this incident:

> Regardless of what Patton knew at the time, Hammelburg
> was the least defensible decision he ever made, and nearly
> as self-destructive as the slappings [described in chapter
> 13]. His denials notwithstanding, the raid not only branded
> Patton a liar but tarnished the very fabric on which his
> fame rested—that his troops came first, and everything
> possible must be done to insure their survival. Instead he

had sent 307 men on a mission whose implicit purpose was the rescue of his own son-in-law.[40]

Blumenson is noncommittal on the question of whether Patton erred in ordering the raid on Hammelburg. He cites the disruptive and destructive nature of the raid on the Germans:

> Task Force Baum disrupted the Aschaffenburg-Hammelburg area, damaged military trains, destroyed antiaircraft guns, upset troop schedules, disabled assault-gun units, provoked general uncertainty and confusion among the Germans, and showed how close the end of the war had come. But would Patton have sent a force to Hammelburg—whether to make a feint or to liberate the prisoners—if he had not thought that Waters was likely to be there?[41]

Perhaps the best analysis of Patton's actions comes from the leader of Task Force Baum himself. In his book *Raid! The Untold Story of Patton's Secret Mission*, Abe Baum wrote:

> Reading Patton's motives is not as easy as it seems. To expose men to peril and death by sending them to rescue a member of his own family seems cruel and selfish. Patton later claimed there were other considerations, some of which were realized though the mission itself failed. And Patton was far from simply a selfish and cruel man. His endurance, stamina and uncomplaining nature, his willingness to do more than was ordered, endeared him to his soldiers. Patton never tired of proving his courage to himself. Perhaps that is why he sent men on the Hammelburg raid—because he would have wanted to go himself....[42]

CHAPTER TEN

SAVING THE LIPIZZANERS

"I ask you, General Patton, and the representatives of the U.S. government to take under your protecting hand this old Austrian Academy, a cultural institution of the noble art of riding, unique in Europe, and perhaps unique in the world."

—COL. PODHASKY, SPANISH RIDING SCHOOL

By late April 1945, as the Nazi army collapsed, there was a panicked flight west of those who sought to escape the advancing Soviet army. German soldiers sought to surrender to the Americans instead, fearing being dispatched to Siberia as slave labor if they were captured by the Russians. POWs also sought to avoid being transferred to the custody of the Russians. One man was on a mission not to save himself or his soldiers but to save his horses—the famous Lipizzaners of the Spanish Riding School. The head of the school, the Austrian army colonel Alois Podhajsky, sought an audience with Lieutenant General Walton Walker, commander of XX Corps, which was part of Patton's Third Army.

Podhajsky pleaded with Walker to save his horses from the Russians, but Walker, though sympathetic, pointed out that there was still a war going on. "I'd like to help but I just can't see how I can right now." A dejected Podhajsky left Walker's office, but on his way back to his camp he ran into an American army major who recognized him as one of the Austrian riders in the 1936 Olympics. At that time the army possessed a number of officers who were horsemen. The major introduced himself. "How are you getting on, Colonel? Is there anything I can do for your horses?"

Podhajsky explained the precarious situation of the Lipizzaners and his fear that if the Russians took the horses they could shipped off to Russia, used as draft animals, or even worse, become food to satisfy the appetites of the Russian soldiers. He explained how he had failed in his plea to the major's commander, General Walker. The major immediately called Walker's headquarters and spoke with an adjutant, impressing upon him that the world's best riding horses were facing extinction.

Walker responded to the renewed plea to save the horses by kicking it up the chain of command. "Maybe we should invite General Patton down here for a show," he said, "and in that way we can get more stars in back of this thing than I've got." Patton accepted the invitation to witness a demonstration of the horses' famous highly choreographed "ballet." The next day Patton motored from his headquarters in southern Germany to Schloss Arco in St. Martin, Upper Austria, to which Podhajsky had evacuated the stallions in January 1945, when air raids threatened Vienna. Patton was accompanied by Undersecretary of War Robert P. Patterson, who was visiting him at the time. Patton may have accepted the invitation to watch the Lipizzaners perform in an attempt to entertain his visiting dignitary. The two Americans were received in imperial style and treated to a dazzling demonstration of the Spanish Riding School's Lipizzaner stallions.

Walker knew that Patton, a lifelong horseman with a growing antipathy to the Russians, would likely be inclined to save the Lipizzaners. Patton had grown up riding. He had played polo, hunted foxes on horseback, and competed in steeplechases. In the 1912 Olympics, he had placed sixth out of twenty-three contestants in the equestrian event. He had also had a long career in the cavalry, writing that a cavalry leader "must have a passion—not simply a liking—for horses, for nothing short of an absorbing passion can make him take the necessary interest in his mount."

After the demonstration, Podhajsky addressed Patton and Patterson. He knew this was his best and perhaps only chance to save his beloved horses. After witnessing the riding demonstration, Patton had mixed emotions. Initially he found it unsettling that amid the greatest conflict the world had ever seen, a group of men had occupied themselves not by picking up arms, but by training show horses. In his diary entry for that day he wrote,

> It struck me as rather strange that, in the midst of a world at war, some twenty young and middle-aged men in great physical condition, together with about thirty grooms, had spent their entire time teaching a group of horses to wriggle their butts and raise their feet in consonance with certain signals from the heels and reins. Much as I like horses, this seemed to me wasted energy.

Given the immense sacrifices made by the Americans he led in liberating Europe, it is not surprising that Patton was mystified that the equine riding school managed to exist in such a bubble during World War II. In fact, given Patton's notorious temper, it is perhaps surprising that he did not erupt at the thought of the horse trainers escaping the violence that the troops he led were forced to endure for their benefit.

Podhajsky halted his horse before Patton and removed his hat in a traditional salute. As he later wrote in his memoirs, "In a little Austrian village in a decisive hour two men faced each other, the one as triumphant conqueror in a war waged with such bitterness, the other as a member of a defeated nation." The forty-seven-year-old Austrian colonel then addressed his invited guest and made his plea:

> General Patton, I am announcing the end of the performance and I thank you and the Honorable Mr. Patterson … as well as all generals for the great honor you have paid this Spanish Imperial Riding Academy by your gracious visit…. I ask you, General Patton, and the representatives of the U.S. government to take under your protecting hand this old Austrian Academy, a cultural institution of the noble art of riding, unique in Europe, and perhaps unique in the world. This school demonstrates the development of culture of the 16th century and it represents the era of the Baroque almost kept intact.

Patton then rose and addressed his Austrian host. The two had much in common. Both were military men, both loved horses, and both had competed in equestrian events in the Olympics. Patton replied that he was putting the Spanish Riding School under the special protection of the United States Army.

He explained his motivation in his diary:

> On the other hand, it is probably wrong to permit any highly developed art, no matter how fatuous, to perish from the earth—and which arts are fatuous depends on the point of view. To me the high-schooling of horses is certainly more interesting than either painting or music.[1]

"This official declaration was far more than I had dreamed," gushed Podhajsky in his memoirs.

OPERATION COWBOY[2]

The rescue of the stallions was not the end of the Lipizzaners' drama. Just days earlier, on April 26, 1945, a German intelligence unit had surrendered to the Second Cavalry Group at a hunting lodge near the Czech border. Some of the German unit's secret documents included photographs of beautiful horses, including Lipizzaners, which came to the attention of Colonel Charles Hancock Reed. The German officer with whom Reed reviewed the photographs explained that the horses were among hundreds that the Germans had collected from the finest breeding stock in Europe and had sent to a large stud farm in the nearby town of Hostau, Czechoslovakia, where Czech and Polish prisoners were caring for them.

Reed was determined not to let the horses fall into the hands of the swiftly approaching Russian army, but he faced one daunting obstacle: the Yalta Agreement. Czechoslovakia was now within the Soviet zone of occupation. Reed sent a message to Third Army headquarters requesting approval for a rescue operation. Patton's quick response: "Get them. Make it fast!"

With the Red Army only about sixty miles east of Hostau, Reed planned a daring rescue. He sent a messenger to the Germans at the stud farm requesting a representative to negotiate terms of surrender. That evening a German officer, Captain Rudolf Lessing, a staff veterinarian at Hostau, approached a Second Cavalry outpost. He was taken to Reed and presented a counterproposal—send an officer back with him to Hostau to confer with the local German commander, and the two men would negotiate a surrender. Reed telephoned Patton and then dispatched Captain Thomas M. Stewart, an intelligence officer with the Second Cavalry's Forty-second Reconnaissance Squadron, to accompany Lessing back to Hostau. Stewart, the son of a U.S. senator from Tennessee, carried a letter in both German and English designating him as the American emissary under Lessing's protection and indicating that he was empowered to negotiate the surrender.

Lessing and Stewart set out on foot and walked for half a mile before coming to the motorcycle that Lessing had hidden in some bushes. They rode to the barn of a friendly Czech, where they exchanged the motorcycle for a pair of horses, setting off again about midnight. The remaining eighteen miles of their journey took them through dense woods—"the forest was so thick through there you felt like you were riding through two walls of darkness," Stewart recalled years later. An experienced rider, Stewart was thrilled to find himself astride a Lipizzaner stallion—a favorite mount of King Peter II of Yugoslavia, no less. When he encountered a three-foot-high road block of logs and branches, the American charged the obstacle intending to jump it. His German guide, who knew a way around the roadblock, called out to Stewart, "He doesn't jump!" It was too late to stop Stewart and his stallion, although the warning was unnecessary—the pair made a perfect leap across the obstacle.

Once they arrived at the stud farm, Stewart encountered a more serious obstacle. The manager of the farm, Lieutenant Colonel Hubert Rudofsky, had initially given his blessing to the plan for surrender but had had a change of heart after Lessing's departure. Rudofsky was a Czech national and he now felt he could negotiate a better deal with the Russians than with the Americans. As Lessing and Stewart approached Lessing's living quarters, they found Lessing's friend and fellow veterinarian Captain Wolfgang Kroll cradling a submachine gun. Rudofsky had told Kroll that if he and Lessing brought in an American, Rudofsky would have the three of them shot as spies.

While Stewart spent the rest of the night nervously crouching in a chair, Lessing sought to determine Rudofsky's whereabouts and disposition. He returned a few hours later, now the morning of April 27, and informed Stewart and Kroll that Rudofsky had left, perhaps to meet with the local army commander, General Schulze. Lessing then set out with Stewart and Kroll, intending to gain an audience with Schulze as well, which they accomplished later that day. Stewart understood enough German to get a sense of what was going on, and it did not seem good. The general sat behind a table surrounded by officers, one of whom, unbeknownst to Stewart, was the silent Lieutenant Colonel Rudofsky. At one point angry words were exchanged, and Lessing replied indignantly, "Sir, I am no spy! I am a German officer. I am no spy!"

The general gestured towards the American officer, who understood this as an invitation to present his credentials. Lessing explained the American's presence, telling the general that their primary responsibility was to the horses. "It is our duty to do everything to save them. It is unimportant for us to win the war here in Hostau on April 27 or 28, 1945. This we should have done four years ago. To do it now is too late."

One of the German officers then said, "Adolf ist kaput." The German general then turned to the American captain and asked, in English, "How many Panzers can you bring?" Stewart understood this as an invitation to a carefully choreographed face-saving ritual of surrender. To surrender when faced with an array of armored tanks bestowed a certain honor on the act, but to surrender to a lone American was ignoble. Stewart assured Schulze that he could return with a sizeable number of tanks and other vehicles. The general stared at Stewart for a long time, then finally scribbled out a note of safe passage for Stewart and assured him that there would be no difficulty for the American troops when they came to Hostau.

Stewart returned to his squadron, accompanied by Kroll, who now insisted on being part of the American advance on the farm. At daybreak the next day, April 28, a task force of two light tanks, two assault guns, and approximately seventy soldiers headed out for Hostau. They reached the farm without incident and found about a hundred Arabian horses, other thoroughbred racing horses and trotters, hundreds of Russian Cossack horses, and some 250 Lipizzaners. In addition to the Czech and Polish POWs they expected, they also found three hundred Americans and as many British prisoners. These were quickly freed.

The task force made preparations to defend the farm from a counterattack. For five hours on April 30 the small force held off an attack from German troops, who had no idea of the surrender that had been negotiated at the farm. The attacking Germans were mainly old men and young boys. The defenders took hundreds of prisoners before the rest of the attackers faded back into the woods. Colonel Reed arrived at the farm on May 1 to inspect the horses and appraise the situation. Before departing, he informed Stewart that the massive German Eleventh Panzer Division would be heading in his direction. "Don't engage them," Reed warned. Only later would Stewart learn the reason, when the entire German division and nine thousand of its soldiers surrendered, as Reed had helped to orchestrate. Two days later, the Third Army liberated the Czech city of Pilsen. Germany surrendered the next day. Reed established his new headquarters at an estate near Pilsen and resolved not to leave until ordered to do so by the U.S. Army, not the Russians.

On May 9, Reed was notified that Patton had approved transporting Colonel Podhajsky to Reed's headquarters, where he could inspect the captured Lipizzaners. With the end of the war in Europe, the Czech and Russian Communists were showing great interest in the captured horses. It was believed that spies had been sent to the stud farm to assess the situation. Reed recommended that the horses be shipped as quickly as possible to central Germany. Third Army headquarters assented, and at dawn on May 12 the movement of the horses began.

With American vehicles positioned in the lead and behind them, and with Polish, Czech, and Cossack riders on each side, a herd of about 350 horses was led away from the advancing Red Army and toward the safety of the American occupying army in southern Germany. The mission, aptly named Operation Cowboy, went quite smoothly. The movement of the horses was given priority along the roads over competing vehicles. All major intersections were closed off ahead of the horses. The fastest group of horses completed the 130-mile journey to Mannsbach in two days. Slower groups arrived a day later. As the horses crossed the border from Czechoslovakia into Germany, they were met by Lieutenant Colonel Rudofsky, who marked the departing animals off a checklist.

A story from the February 1963 issue of *The American Legion* magazine tells how the convoy encountered some trouble as it attempted to cross the border:

"You can't take these horses out of Czechoslovakia," the spokesman for the Allied Commission said. "They must remain there until we decide with the Russians as to just how they should be disposed of."

"Man, you're crazy," the captain told him. "As soon as Ivan finds these horses they're gone—"

"I'm sorry," the civilian shrugged, "but I can't permit you to—"

"Chum," the captain said, "just stop talking and get out of our way.... When General Patton tells you to do something you do it."

According to this account, when Patton was told there was a problem at the border, he exploded. "The German Army didn't stop us, and no darn group of civilians is going to do it, that's for sure."[3]

On the afternoon of May 14, Podhajsky arrived at Colonel Reed's headquarters. The two men met over dinner. Reed surprised the Austrian by telling him that he watched him compete in the 1936 Olympics in Berlin. Reed was a member of the U.S. Army's riding team and had been so impressed by Podhajsky that he had named one of the cavalry school horses after him. The next morning the two men traveled by jeep to Mannsbach, where Podhajsky identified the Lipizzaners belonging to the Austrian herd so that they could be sent to St. Martin. Before departing, Podhajsky attempted to thank the American for all he had done to save the Lipizzaners. "I have only acted as a fellow rider should," Reed replied. "And I am convinced that you would have done the same if the positions were reversed."

A little over a week later, a convoy of captured German trucks pulled up to an abandoned airfield outside of St. Martin. The trucks carried 226 Lipizzaners that were being returned to Austria. To show his appreciation for all the Americans had done for his beloved horses, Podhajsky staged performances for the American soldiers over the next several months. Patton attended his second performance on August 21, 1945. Thousands of GIs witnessed the shows. "The success of the Lipizzaner with the American Army General was repeated also with the ordinary soldiers," Podhajsky noted proudly. "They were all captivated."

In 1963 the Walt Disney Company released a film about the saving of the Lipizzaners, *Miracle of the White Stallions*. The film, which included depictions of both Patton and Podhajsky, was shot mainly in Vienna, and Colonel Podhajsky choreographed the horses' performance. The movie's serious theme of evil and ignorance threatening a centuries-old culture and long-held values was a departure from Disney's usual fare in the 1960s (*The Absent-Minded Professor, Son of Flubber,* and *The Love Bug*). *Miracle of the White Stallions* popularized the story of Patton's role in saving the beautiful white horses.

Ultimately the saving of the Lipizzaner horses amidst the crushing cruelty of World War II demonstrates a recurring irony of human behavior—we sometimes display our greatest humanity not by how we treat each other, but by how we treat animals. When Colonel Reed was asked to explain the risks undertaken to save the Lipizzaner horses, the bravery of the soldiers involved, and the personal sacrifices made, he provided a starkly clear and insightful answer: "We were so tired of death and destruction, we wanted to do something beautiful." After retiring from the army, Reed purchased an offspring of one of the horses he had rescued and rode the animal every day for nearly thirty years.

Later that year, when Patton sustained what turned out to be fatal injuries in a car crash, a highly regarded neurosurgeon, R. Glen Spurling, was flown to Heidelberg to tend the general. A fifty-one-year-old Kentuckian who had left his practice in Louisville shortly after Pearl Harbor to serve his country, Spurling was assigned to Europe as one of two chief neurosurgical consultants during the war.[4]

Spurling accompanied Patton's wife, Beatrice, on board a C-54 aircraft across the Atlantic. His first examination of the general took place on December 12, 1945, at 4:00 p.m. He found that Patton, while severely injured, was not yet at the point of no return. The prognosis changed drastically over the next fourteen hours. At 10:00 the following morning, Patton's breathing was much more labored and the patient seemed to have lost whatever gains he had made since his initial injury. When Spurling left Patton's bedside, the prognosis was now "increasingly grave."

A short time later, Patton had the neurosurgeon paged. When he returned to the general's room, the two men were alone. "Sit down, Colonel," Patton said. After exchanging pleasantries, Patton came to the point. "Now, Spurling, we've known each other during the fighting and I want you to talk with me as man to man. What chance have I to recover?"

"You're doing so much better than the usual patient with a cervical cord injury that it is impossible to give you a forthright answer," Spurling responded evasively. Patton then posed a more direct question that perhaps captured metaphorically whether he would desire to live or die. "Okay, but what chance have I to ride a horse again?" Patton asked.

"None," Spurling replied with hesitation.

"In other words," Patton said, "the best I could hope for would be semi-invalidism?"

"Yes," Spurling said.

Patton paused for a moment, perhaps contemplating his own will to live. "Thank you, Colonel, for being honest."

Patton's first memory as a child was of horses. His father had taken him to a corral to look at some Shetland ponies, and Patton was able to choose one, a horse he named Peach Blossom. Nine days after being informed he could never ride a horse again, at 5:45 p.m. on December 21, 1945, Patton died in his sleep.

PART III

PRAYER

Better known for his profanity than for his prayers, George Patton was actually a devout and religious man. His profanity was merely a device to capture the attention of his soldiers. Patton's prayers, however, reflected his deep and sincere faith in God. Throughout his life he prayed daily and attended church almost every Sunday, even in wartime.

One cannot read Patton's diaries, letters, speeches, and personal papers without being struck by the frequency with which he appeals to God and turns to the Bible for inspiration. Patton prayed to do his best, he prayed for solace in times of trouble, and he prayed for victory in times of war. "No one can live under the awful responsibility that I have without Divine help," he wrote. In his many trials, Patton turned to God and found remarkable serenity.

The public Patton was brash, self-confident, and boastful. In his private supplications to God, however, a different Patton emerges— humble, uncertain, and seeking guidance. For Patton, God was not a distant and impersonal being but a companion with whom he had a personal relationship. And whenever he achieved anything important, whether it was his admission to West Point or a victory in battle, Patton always gave thanks to God.

For the first twelve years of his life, Patton was educated at home. His aunt read to him three to four hours a day. Her fundamental textbook was the Bible. She also read to him from John Bunyan's Christian allegory, *The Pilgrim's Progress*. He sat beside her in church each Sunday as she recited the liturgical responses from the Book of Common Prayer, and he developed an amazing capacity to repeat passages at length.

Patton's religious beliefs, like the man himself, were unique and defy easy characterization. He was a communicant of the Episcopal Church, but he studied the Koran and the Bhagavad Gita. He was ecumenical in his beliefs, writing that "God was probably indifferent in the way he was approached," but he opposed his daughter's marriage to a Roman Catholic. He was in most respects a traditional Christian, but he had an unshakeable belief in reincarnation and asserted that he had lived former lives throughout history—always as a soldier.

To be successful, Patton believed, a man must plan, work hard, and pray. A man prays to God for assistance in circumstances that he cannot foresee or control. Patton believed that without prayer, his soldiers would "crack up" under the unrelenting pressures of battle. Prayer does not have to take place in church, but can be offered anywhere. Praying, he said, is "like plugging in on a current whose source is in Heaven." Prayer "completes the circuit. It is power."

To Patton, prayer was a "force multiplier"—when combined with or employed by a combat force, it substantially increases the effectiveness of human efforts and enhances the odds of victory. In this sense, prayer was no different from training, leadership, technology, or firepower. But Patton's faith was not a mere contrivance with which he cynically tried to motivate his men. He was a sincere believer. He even directed his chief chaplain to send out a training letter to every unit in the Third Army on the importance of prayer.

Those familiar with Patton's biography are probably already acquainted with the prayer for fair weather that he issued to the soldiers of the Third Army at Christmas in 1944. But few people realized that there are three competing versions of how the prayer came about—two of them by chaplains of the Third Army who both claim authorship. In any case, the Battle of the Bulge was also not the first time that Patton had prayed for good weather for battle.

Patton's life and achievements combined a genius for war, a deep spiritual faith, and a belief in his own destiny. He was no saint, and his strong personality sometimes emphasized his character flaws. But when his country confronted its greatest peril from unspeakable evil, George S. Patton Jr. embodied the strength of character, force of will, and faith in God required to vanquish it.

CHAPTER ELEVEN

GROWING UP

"A man must recognize his destiny. If he does not recognize it, then he is lost."

—PATTON

Soon after his birth, Patton developed the croup. Fearing that he would die unchristened, his nurse, a devout Irish Catholic woman named Mary Scally, secretly baptized him by sprinkling water on his brow when she was alone with the child.[1,2] He was eventually re-baptized into his family's Episcopal church. The Pattons had been Episcopalians from the time of George's great-great-grandfather, Robert Patton, who served as a vestryman of St. George's Episcopal Church in Fredericksburg, Virginia.

As a child, Georgie Patton would get on his knees beside his mother's chair to recite his nightly prayers before going to bed. On the wall behind her hung two portraits. One was a somber man with white hair and beard. The other figure was also bearded but younger and with brown hair. Young Patton assumed they were God and

Jesus. With upturned eyes, he would look at these faces while he prayed. On his seventh birthday, Patton announced that instead of becoming a fireman, he would become a soldier when he grew up. Eventually he learned that the two figures he had prayed before were not God and Jesus but Robert E. Lee and Stonewall Jackson.[3] Years later, Patton would half-jokingly speculate that the notion of a military career had been inspired by his nightly prayers before these two portraits.

Patton's aunt Annie Wilson read to him three to four hours a day from the Bible. She told the boy that the Old Testament was a "manual of survival" which told "the folklore and history of a tough and single-minded race who had survived every kind of persecution from gods and men." When she read from the New Testament and discussed it with Georgie, she portrayed Jesus as a hero in the context of Roman history. She also read to him from John Bunyan's Christian allegory, *The Pilgrim's Progress*. As she sat beside him at church each Sunday, Annie, known as Aunt Nannie, recited aloud from the Book of Common Prayer along with the preacher.[4]

Aunt Nannie had been in love with Patton's father. She was prettier than her sister, Ruth, and thought to be more intelligent, and when George S. Patton II chose to marry her sister, Nannie was devastated. As the newlyweds boarded a train for their honeymoon in New Orleans, Nannie arrived unexpectedly at the station, luggage in hand. She was somehow persuaded that a chaperone was unnecessary. According to family lore, the diary that Nannie had kept faithfully until that night was left blank and never resumed.[5]

The Pattons' honeymoon was to be one of the few occasions that Nannie was not part of their life. With the birth of Georgie, Nannie poured her unrequited love for his father into the son.

In her memoirs many years later, Ruth Ellen Patton reflected on Aunt Nannie's role in the household:

[I]n the 1870s, both the Wilson girls... fell in love with... young George Patton... [who] chose Ruth Wilson.... When the Pattons finally built their own home in 1900, Aunt Nannie... moved right in with them. So, all her life she lived in the house with the only man she had ever loved and she lived vicariously in his son, Georgie.[6]

Growing up, Patton dreaded with great anxiety that he would "get the Call"—an irresistible divine summons to the ministry. Every night he would dutifully pray to Jesus not to call him because he wanted to be a soldier.[7] As he grew older, his ambition grew to be not just a soldier but a great soldier, and he was willing to subjugate even his gentle nature to achieve it. In his journal he wrote, "Remember you have placed all on war.... Therefore you must never fail.... If you do not die a soldier and having had a chance to be one I pray to God to dam [sic] you George Patton.... Never Never Never stop being ambitious. You have but one life. Live it to the full of glory and be willing to pay." His ambition was consistent with one of his favorite biblical verses, Proverbs 23:7: "For as he thinketh in his heart, so is he."[8]

Patton had an overwhelming sense that he had a destiny to fulfill. While at West Point he wrote to his father, "I know that my ambition is selfish and cold yet it is not a selfishness [sic] for instead of sparing me, it makes me exert my self.... Of course I may be a dreamer but I have a firm conviction I am not and in any case I will do my best to attain what I consider—wrongly perhaps—my destiny."[9]

That destiny, he believed, was guided by a higher power. In another letter to his father from West Point, Patton wrote:

Now don't think that I don't like the army for... it is the only place I would be worth a darn. But either I must get into another army and fight or else wait until the trampled

worm [the United States] turns into an avenging dragon....
This sounds funny from a person who has never yet done
anything but God willing I can and, given the chance, I will
carve my name on something bigger than a section room
bench.[10]

Patton recognized that in order to fulfill his destiny he needed the
intervention of God to provide a war in which he could exercise his
talents. In a letter to Beatrice, his future wife, he wrote from West
Point:

Now this is a rash thing to say and if twenty years from now
with no war and no promotions someone should say, "I
thought you were going to teach the world?" why it would
hurt. But if there were no dreamers I honestly think there
would be little advance and even dreams may, no must,
come true if a man gives his life for what he believes. Of
course it is hard for anyone particularly for me who has
never done much to give reasons why he believes in myself
but foolish as it seems I do believe in myself.... I know that
if there is a war "which God grant" I will make a name or
at worse an end.[11]

In 1927, when his aging father was near death, Patton recalled how
his father had fueled his belief that fate guided his son's footsteps:

He had always expressed to me his belief that the very
fortunate career I had had in the army was Fate and that I
was being specially prepared for some special work. He and
Mr. Gaffey felt that the end of our Civilization was at hand
and that war was sure. When I used to bemoan the fact that

wars were getting scarce and that all the time I had spent
getting ready would be wasted for lack of opportunity he
used to assure me with the greatest confidence that I would
yet be in the greatest war in history. He was most convinc-
ing and I believed him, particularly as I have always felt
the same thing concerning myself....[12]

"A man must know his destiny," Patton believed. "If he does not recognize it, then he is lost. By this I mean, once, twice, or at the very
most, three times, fate will reach out and tap a man on the shoulder.
If he has the imagination, he will turn around and fate will point out
to him what fork in the road he should take, if he has the guts, he will
take it."[13]

Beatrice too believed that her husband was destined for some great
achievement. On December 2, 1942, she wrote:

I feel, as you do, that all your life has pointed to this and
that you still have many big things ahead, and that God is
with you and guiding your every move. I can't even think
about your personal ambition or promotion any more than
you can, for I feel sure that you are marked by destiny and
that I am willing to wait on God for that.[14]

Patton once described himself as "a passenger floating on a river
of destiny."[15] Although events during World War II occasionally tested
his belief in his divinely ordained destiny, he always returned to it.
After a treacherous flight in North Africa in which his aircraft came
perilously close to hitting a mountain, Patton said he was frightened
"until I thought of my destiny. That calmed me."[16] Before the invasion
of Sicily, when he was forced into a role subordinate to the British
commander General Bernard L. Montgomery, Patton retained his

self-confidence, writing, "I have greater ability than these other people and it comes from, for lack of a better word, what we must call greatness of soul based on a belief—an unshakable belief—in my destiny."[17]

Although he was a devout Christian throughout his life, Patton was also very interested in other religions. During the Punitive Expedition in Mexico, Patton first met Mormons. Some Mexican bandits were harassing American Mormons who had built farms across the border, and the U.S. troops were escorting those who wished to leave. Patton borrowed a copy of the Book of Mormon from one of the faithful and read it with great interest. One of the families he protected was that of Bishop Crow. Patton said that the "old procreator" had four wives at least, because every time he went to escort a Mrs. Crow across the border, it was a different lady.[18]

Decades later, while stationed in Hawaii, the Pattons were invited to a party thrown by the Mormons on the windward side of Oahu to celebrate the visit of some church elders from Salt Lake City. Mrs. Patton was seated near the head of the table near a taciturn and sour-looking elder whom she could not engage in small talk. Finally she noted the name on his place card and said hopefully, "Are you by any chance related to that nice Bishop Crow and his lovely wives that Colonel Patton escorted out of Mexican territory in 1914 when we were having trouble with Pancho Villa?" The surprised elder turned to her and said, "He was my father, madam, but Bishop Crow is now one of the Twelve Apostles." When her husband tried to explain that the "Twelve Apostles" referred to the governing body of the Mormon Church, Mrs. Patton waved him away, not wanting to spoil the thrill that she had evidently entertained about sitting next to the son of one of Christ's disciples.[19]

CHAPTER TWELVE

GOD OF BATTLES

*"No one can live under the awful responsibility that I have
without Divine help."*

—PATTON

O n August 23, 1923, during a summer vacation at his in-laws'
beachfront estate in Massachusetts, Patton and his wife went
sailing in a two-person runabout. They heard cries for help
from three small boys whose boat had overturned. They raced over
to the boys who were in the water waving their arms. When they
hauled the boys into the boat, Patton's tiny sailboat hung dangerously
low in the water. His wife urged him to drop the sail and row home,
thinking it would be safer than risking capsizing by sailing. Patton
felt the boys would catch pneumonia if they did not get to shore
quickly. "We must sail!" Patton declared, "I've done all I can, and if
there is anyone in this boat worth saving, the Lord will have to help
us now." The boat reached the shore safely.[1]

Patton received the Life Saving Medal of Honor from the Trea-
sury Department for rescuing the boys. One of his best friends,

Walter Dillingham, wrote to congratulate Patton: "I am prepared to decorate the whole family for bravery on general principles, but I had always thought of your special forte as being one of killing rather than saving lives. It must be a fine sensation to know that one is a well rounded hero."[2]

The incident captures Patton's lifelong belief that in any moment of danger, whether it be a violent engagement with the enemy on a battlefield or a moment of personal danger in a sailboat, the Lord would protect him. In countless journal entries, personal letters, and conversations, he unfailingly spoke of placing his destiny in the hands of God.

The American and British invasion of French North Africa, known as Operation Torch, began on November 8, 1942. The Allies' plan was to invade northwest Africa—Morocco, Algeria, and Tunisia—and advance eastward to attack German forces from behind. The invasion was split into three different task forces—Western, Center, and Eastern. Patton headed the Western Task Force, targeting Casablanca. Before the Operation Torch landings in North Africa in 1942, Patton wrote the following in his diary:

> In forty hours I shall be in battle, with little information, and on the spur of the moment will have to make most momentous decisions, but I believe that one's spirit enlarges with responsibility and that, with God's help, I shall make them and make them right. It seems that my whole life has been pointed to this moment. When this job is done, I presume I will be pointed to the next step in the ladder of destiny. If I do my duty, the rest will take care of itself.

The invasion was a success, and Patton was soon promoted to major general.

Giving thanks to God was also a ritual Patton faithfully observed. After the successful landing of his task force in Morocco in Novem-

ber 1942, Patton wrote that he was forced to believe that his "proverbial luck or more probably the direct intervention of the Lord was
responsible." He then addressed a letter to all of his commanding
officers:

> It is my firm conviction that the great success attending the
> hazardous operations carried out on sea and on land by the
> Western Task Force could only have been possible through
> the intervention of Divine Providence manifested in many
> ways. Therefore, I should be pleased if, in so far as circum-
> stances and conditions permit, our grateful thanks be
> expressed today in appropriate religious services.[3]

In his diary entry for November 22, 1942, Patton noted that he
went to church. "Keyes[4] and I went to mass this morning. I at least
had reason to take a little time off to thank God. There were quite a
lot of widows, made by us, in the church. They cried a good deal but
did not glare at us."

Patton turned to God for help in dealing not only with the enemy
but also with his own senior commanders and allies. Patton's aggressive style of warfare sometimes produced friction with his superiors,
who often insisted on a slower, more cautious approach. He also
fought over allocations of supplies between competing army groups.
Before meetings to discuss strategy, Patton would enlist God's support
for his approach. As he wrote to Beatrice on August 21, 1944,

> We jumped seventy miles to day and took Sens, Montereau,
> and Melun so fast the bridges were not blown. If I can keep
> on the way I want to go I will be quite a fellow....
>
> We are going so fast that I am quite safe. My only worries
> are my relations and not my enemies.
>
> Well I will stop and read the Bible so as to be ready to have
> celestial help in my argument tomorrow to keep moving.[5]

On February 4, 1945, he wrote to her, "You may hear that I am on the defensive but it was not the enemy who put me there. I don't see much future for me in this war. There are too many 'safety first' people running it. However, I have felt this way before and something has always turned up. I will go to church and see what can be done...."

Sometimes his superiors' resistance to his aggressive strategy and the competition from his British allies for supplies seemed to equal what he had to contend with from the enemy. He confided to Beatrice in September 1944, "If I only had the Germans to fight, it would be a cinch.... God deliver us from our friends. We can handle the enemy."[6]

Patton had faith in the comforting power of Scripture. On D-Day, while he waited impatiently for his opportunity to join the action, he wrote to Beatrice,

> Ike broadcast to occupied Europe and did it well.
>
> None of the troops of this army are in yet and in fact I doubt if the enemy knows of its existence. We will try to give him quite a surprise....
>
> I can't tell when I will go in.... However I have had my bag packed for some time just in case.
>
> It is Hell to be on the side lines and see all the glory eluding me, but I guess there will be enough for all....
>
> I guess I will read the Bible.[7]

In his own provocative way, Patton once encouraged his friend General Johnny Lucas to read the Bible. Before the landings at Anzio, Italy, in January 1944, which Lucas led, Patton advised him, "John, there is no one in this Army I hate to see killed as much as you, but you can't get out of this alive. Of course, you might only be wounded. No one ever blames a wounded general for anything." Patton instructed the worried Lucas to "read the Bible when the going gets tough." Then Patton took one of his aides aside and said, apparently seriously, "Look here, if things get too bad, shoot the old man in the back end, but don't you dare kill the old bastard." After Lucas found out about the remark, he admitted being afraid to turn his back on Patton from D-Day on.[8]

It was impossible, Patton believed, to bear the burden of command and the incomparable stresses of war without divine guidance:

> Went to church.... [W]e had a new preacher, at my insistence, who was good. He preached on the willingness to accept responsibility, even to your own hurt. That ability is what we need and what Ike lacks. But I do feel that I don't. I pray daily to do my duty, retain my self-confidence, and accomplish my destiny. No one can live under the awful responsibility that I have without Divine help. Frequently I feel that I don't rate it.[9]

Though Patton assured his troops that biblical teachings were fully consistent with their mission to kill the enemy, he privately conceded the difficulty of reconciling the essential message of Christianity with the terrible exigencies of warfare. Recalling the first mass he attended in Europe after the D-Day landings, Patton wrote in his diary, "As we knelt in the mud in the slight drizzle, we could distinctly hear the roar of the guns, and the whole sky was filled with airplanes on their missions of destruction... quite at variance with the teachings of the religion we were practicing." The French countryside was dotted with crossroad crucifixes, which the Army Signal Corps found useful as makeshift telephone poles. "While the crosses were in no way injured," Patton recorded, "I could not help thinking of the incongruity of the lethal messages passing over the wires."

D'Este has described Patton's most dreadful challenge:

> how to motivate decent young men raised on the precepts
> of the Bible, the sanctity of human life, and the immorality

of killing to become an efficient cog in a gigantic killing machine such as an armored division. While it was enough to make their mothers cringe, the only method whereby a Patton... could succeed on a battlefield was to trespass on the inherent decency of Americans by training and motivating their men to survive by killing others whose task was to kill them. Patton did it as well or better than virtually anyone else.

Patton sought to overcome his troops' reluctance to kill with a dramatic motivational speech that he had composed himself and would deliver from memory. The speech became his trademark. It comprised elements of Scripture, chivalry, poetry, and the principles of war. "The only good enemy is a dead enemy," he assured his men. "Misses do not kill, but a bullet in the heart or a bayonet in the guts does.... Battle is not a terrifying ordeal to be endured. It is a magnificent experience wherein all the elements that have made man superior to the beasts are present: courage, self-sacrifice, loyalty, help to others, devotion to duty."

"Patton," the editor of his personal papers writes, "never lost sight of his ultimate goal, to prepare his men for combat. He concentrated on teaching his men to kill efficiently, instinctively. He presented a speaker with these words: 'Men, I want to introduce to you the noblest work of God—a killer!'"[10]

CHAPLAINS

Patton thought chaplains were essential to his army's effectiveness in combat, and he pushed them as hard as any other soldiers under his command. "He wanted a chaplain to be above average in courage, leadership and example, particularly the example of his life," the Third Army's head chaplain, Monsignor James H. O'Neill, remembered.

"And in time of battle, he wanted the chaplains up front, where the men were dying. And that's where the Third Army chaplains went—up front. We lost more chaplains, proportionately, than any other group." Patton's insistence on discipline and standards of dress also applied to the chaplains and the services they conducted. All chaplains had to be neatly uniformed, the altars appropriately arranged and the services orderly. The men needed to be at their best when "talking with God."[11]

The greatest failing of a chaplain in Patton's eyes was not tending to front-line troops who were wounded or dying. On a visit to the 47th Regiment, Patton cursed the chaplain for not being at the front with his troops. An eyewitness to the one-sided exchange observed, "When I say cussed, I mean he used every bit of invective in his expansive vocabulary."[12]

In the speech that he used so effectively to motivate and inspire his troops, Patton paid his peculiar homage to the chaplains:

> Every single man in the Army plays a vital part. Every little job is essential to the whole scheme. What if every truck driver suddenly decided that he didn't like the whine of those shells and turned yellow and jumped headlong into a ditch? He could say to himself, "They won't miss me—just one guy in thousands." What if every man said that? Where in the hell would we be now? No, thank God, Americans don't say that. Every man does his job. Every man serves the whole. Every department, every unit is important to the vast scheme of things. The Ordnance is needed to supply the guns, the Quartermaster is needed to bring up the food and clothes for us—for where we are going there isn't a hell of a lot to steal. Every last damn man in the mess hall, even the one who heats the water to keep us from getting diarrhea, has a job to do. Even the Chaplain is important, for if we get killed and he is not there to bury us, we would all go to hell.[13]

The chaplains' efforts on behalf of his army were not merely incidental. Monsignor O'Neill recalled that the most impressive speech he ever witnessed was Patton's announcement to his senior commanders of his plans for the counterattack during the Battle of the Bulge. Standing in front of a large map, Patton described the ninety-degree turn by which the Third Army would stop the German advance and rescue the 101st Airborne, which was encircled at Bastogne:

> Gentlemen, this is a hell of a Christmas present, but it was handed to me and I pass it on to you. Tonight the Third Army turns and attacks north. I would have much preferred to have continued our attack to the east as planned, but I am a soldier. I fight where I am told, and I win where I fight! There is one encouraging factor in our favor, however. The bastards will be easier to kill coming at us above ground than they would be skulking in their holes. You have all done a grand job so far, but I expect more of you now.[14]

As Patton concluded, he suddenly looked to the back of the large room and cried out, "Padre, are you back there?"

"Yes, sir," replied a surprised O'Neill.
"Now you get to work," barked Patton.[15]

Courage was a virtue that Patton carefully cultivated as a cadet, as a young officer, and throughout his life. He constantly challenged himself and tested his own courage. His favorite description of courage came from his personal chaplain, the Episcopalian George R. Metcalf, who joined the Third Army in November 1944 as assistant head chaplain: "Courage is fear that has said its prayers."[16]

Prior to World War II, Patton was posted to Fort Myer in Virginia, near Washington, D.C. A regular churchgoer, he summoned the chaplain and bluntly told him that his sermons were too long. "I don't yield to any man in my reverence to the Lord, but God damn it, no sermon needs to take longer than ten minutes. I'm sure you can make your point in that time." The following Sunday Patton sat in the front pew. When the chaplain began his sermon, Patton ostentatiously took out his watch. Not surprisingly, the chaplain concluded his sermon exactly ten minutes later.[17]

Patton made the same point a few years later, after the invasion of Sicily: "I had all the non-Catholic chaplains in the other day and gave them hell for having uninteresting services.... I told them that I was going to relieve any preacher who talked more than ten minutes on any subject. I will probably get slapped down by the Church union."[18]

He would not tolerate defeatism in prayers or sermons. Preachers who committed that particular sin he called "pulpit killers." Clergymen who insisted "thou shalt not kill" knew less about the Bible than he did, Patton argued. He insisted it was not a sin to kill if one served on the side of God, citing the Old Testament story of David slaying Goliath. Patton would swiftly communicate his displeasure at sermons that dwelt on death or families whose sons would never return home. Instead he demanded sermons and prayers which emphasized courage and victory.[19]

Confident in his own religious convictions and his knowledge of the Bible, Patton did not hesitate publicly to contradict a chaplain's sermon, as this diary entry for Armistice Day, 1943, reveals:

> We went to a Memorial Service at the cemetery at 1100. The Chaplain preached a sermon on sacrifice and the usual bull, so as I put the wreath at the foot of the flagpole, I said, "I consider it no sacrifice to die for my country. In my mind we came here to thank God that men like these have lived rather than to regret that they have died."[20]

Coy Eklund, an officer on Patton's staff, confirms a story about Patton's insistence on inspirational sermons:

> It is no myth that one Sunday morning, after attending church services as he always did, he stalked into my office in the Army barracks in Nancy, France, where I was the senior duty officer.
>
> "Eklund," he demanded, "do you know Chaplain So-and-so?"
>
> "Yes, sir," I replied.
>
> "Well get rid of the son of a bitch. He can't preach!"
>
> And we got rid of him.[21]

Patton himself tells a similar story in his diary entry for November 12, 1944: "Went to church where I heard the worst service yet. Sent for the Chief of Chaplains to have the offender removed and get a new chaplain...."[22]

He was not always unhappy with his chaplains' preaching, however. The biographer Martin Blumenson describes an episode during the Third Army's breakout across France: "Patton went to church with the black troops of a quartermaster truck battalion. The dignity of the service and the music by the choir were impressive. 'The colored preacher preached the best sermon I have ever heard during this war.'"[23] Given the standards to which Patton held his chaplains, that was high praise indeed.

REINCARNATION

Although George Patton was a devout Christian, he also believed in reincarnation. From childhood he had a sense of prior lives that seemed to be more than a mere heightened sense of déjà vu and not just the product of his extensive study of history. His past lives extended across a number of historical periods, but there was one constant—he was always a soldier. Patton believed that after he died he would one day be reborn to lead men in battle.

One of Patton's favorite poems was Wordsworth's "Ode on Intimations of Immortality from Recollections of Early Childhood," with its theme of an everlasting soul:

> Our birth is but a sleep and a forgetting:
> The Soul that rises with us, our life's Star,
> Hath elsewhere its setting,
> And cometh from afar:
> Not in entire forgetfulness,
> And not in utter nakedness,
> But trailing clouds of glory do we come
> From God, who is our home:
> Heaven lies about us in our infancy!

As a boy, Patton organized an "attack," enlisting his young cousins to take an abandoned farm wagon, which they hauled to the top of a small hill. The boys crouched in the wagon, imagining their sticks were spears and arrows and clutching the lids of wooden wine barrels for shields. As the wagon careened down the hill, it encountered its unsuspecting "enemy," a flock of turkeys. Several of the enemy were killed and mangled. When his mother asked him what in the world he was doing, George replied that he was copying the famous war wagons of John the Blind of Bohemia, who won many victories this way in the fifteenth century. How did the boy know this? "Oh, I was there," he answered. The boy's mysterious response did not spare him from punishment for the destruction of the turkeys.[24]

D'Este describes an occasion in World War I when Patton "remembered" an incident from a past life:

> Patton was ordered to a secret destination in a part of France where he had never been.... [N]ear the top of a hill Patton leaned forward and asked his driver "if the camp wasn't out of sight just over the hill and to the right. The driver replied, 'No sir... but there is an old Roman camp over there to the right....'" As Patton was leaving the camp he asked an officer: "Your theater is over here straight ahead isn't it?" The officer responded, "We have no theater here, but... there is an old Roman theater only about three hundred yards away."[25]

Patton's grandson remembered conversations about reincarnation. "If discussing reincarnation (one of his favorite topics), he would offer up as evidence pertinent bits of the Bhagavad Gita[26] ('For sure is the death of him that is born, and sure the birth of him that is dead'), and his old standby, Revelation 3:12: 'Him that overcometh will I make a pillar in the temple of my God, and he shall go no more out.'"[27]

PATTON'S POETRY

"What manner of man was this who took equal pleasure and pride in writing a poem and in killing an enemy soldier with his pistol?" asks Martin Blumenson. Patton had a lifelong interest in literature, including poetry. Kipling appears to have been his favorite poet. Throughout his campaigns in World War II, Patton carried with him a Bible, the Book of Common Prayer, Caesar's *Commentaries*, and a complete set of Kipling's poetry. He could quote poetry appropriate for a variety of occasions.

Patton wrote poetry for most of his adult life. The most common themes of his compositions are bawdiness, chivalry, religion, and warfare, and sometimes all of these themes appear in one work. His poetry is of mixed quality, and is best appreciated as an unvarnished expression of his philosophy of life and war, offering insights into his character and beliefs. "Through a Glass Darkly," [28] which he wrote in 1922, deals with the soul, reincarnation, and God.

Through the travail of the ages
Midst the pomp and toil of war
Have I fought and strove and perished
Countless times upon this star.
In the form of many peoples
In all panoplies of time
Have I seen the luring vision
Of the victory Maid sublime.
I have battled for fresh mammoth
I have warred for pastures new
I have listened to the whispers
When the race track instinct grew.
I have known the call to battle
In each changeless changing shape
From the high-souled voice of conscience
To the beastly lust for rape.
I have sinned and I have suffered
Played the hero and the knave
Fought for the belly, shame or country
And for each have found a grave.
I cannot name my battles
For the visions are not clear
Yet I see the twisted faces

And feel the rending spear.
Perhaps I stabbed our Saviour
In his sacred helpless side.
Yet I've called His name in blessing
When in after times I died.
In the dimness of the shadows
Where we hairy heathens warred
I can taste in thought the life blood—
We used teeth before the sword.
While in later clearer vision
I can sense the coppery sweat
Feel the pikes grow wet and slippery
Where our phalanx Cyrus met.
Hear the rattle of the harness
Where the Persian darts bounced clear
See the chariots wheel in panic
From the Hoplite leveled spear.
See the mole grow monthly longer
Reaching for the walls of Tyre
Hear the crash of tons of granite
Smell the quenchless eastern fire.
Still more clearly as a Roman
Can I see the Legion close
As our third rank moved in forward
And the short sword found our foes.
Once again I feel the anguish
Of that blistering treeless plain
When the Parthian showered death bolts
And our discipline was in vain.
I remember all the suffering
Of those arrows in my neck
Yet I stabbed a grinning savage

As I died upon my back.
Once again I smell the heat sparks
When my Flemish plate gave way
And the lance ripped through my entrails
As on Crecy's field I lay.
In the windless blinding stillness
Of the glittering tropic sea
I can see the bubbles rising
Where we set the captives free.
Midst the spume of half a tempest
I have heard the bulwarks go
When the crashing, point-blank round shot
Sent destruction to our foe.
I have fought with gun and cutlass
On the red and slippery deck
With all Hell aflame within me
And a rope around my neck.
And still later as a general
Have I galloped with Murat
While we laughed at death and numbers
Trusting in the Emperor's star.
Till at last our star had faded
And we shouted to our doom
Where the sunken road of Ohain
Closed us in its quivering gloom.
So but now with Tanks aclatter
Have I waddled on the foe
Belching death at twenty paces
By the starshell's ghastly glow.
So as through a glass and darkly
The age long strife I see
Where I fought in many guises,

Many names—but always me.
And when I see not in my blindness
What the objects were I wrought
But as God rules o'er our bickerings
It was through His will I fought.
So for ever in the future
Shall I battle as of yore,
Dying to be born a fighter
But to die again once more.

GOD OF OUR FATHERS
From Patton's speech to the Second Armored Division, December 1941

I shall be delighted to lead you against any enemy, confident in the fact that your disciplined valor and high training will bring victory.

Put your heart and soul into being expert killers with your weapons. The only good enemy is a dead enemy. Misses do not kill, but a bullet in the heart or a bayonet in the guts do. Let every bullet find its billet—it is the body of your foes.... Battle is not a terrifying ordeal to be endured. It is a magnificent experience wherein all the elements that have made man superior to the beasts are present: courage, self-sacrifice, loyalty, help to others, devotion to duty.

Remember that these enemies, whom we shall have the honor to destroy, are good soldiers and stark fighters. To beat such men, you must not despise their ability, but you must be confident in your own superiority.... Remember too that your God is with you.

God of our Fathers, known of old,
Lord of our far-flung battle-line,
Beneath whose awful Hand we hold
Dominion over palm and pine...[29]

The earth is full of anger,
The seas are dark with wrath,
The Nations in their harness
Go up against our path:
Ere yet we loose the legions—
Ere yet we draw the blade,
Jehovah of the Thunders,
Lord God of Battles, aid!

. . . .

E'en now their vanguard gathers,
E'en now we face the fray—
As Thou didst help our fathers,
Help Thou our host today!
Fulfilled of signs and wonders,
In life, in death made clear—
Jehovah of the Thunders,
Lord God of Battles, hear![30]

The inexperienced American army's first major encounter with the Germans resulted in a resounding defeat at the Kasserine Pass in Tunisia. On February 14, 1943, Rommel's Tenth and Twenty-first Panzer Divisions of the Afrika Korps launched an attack against the U.S. position. The II Corps, under the command of Major General Lloyd Fredendall, was driven back twenty-one miles in nine days. One hundred ninety-two men were killed, 2,624 wounded, and 2,459 were captured or went missing. The encounter seemed to confirm Hitler's contempt for the battle-worthiness of American soldiers.

Two weeks later, Patton took over command of II Corps from Fredendall and wrote this letter to the troops now under his command:

All of us have been in battle. But due to circumstances beyond the control of anyone, we have heretofore fought separately. In our next battle we shall, for the first time on this continent, have many thousands of Americans united in one command.... In union there is strength!

Our duty... is plain. We must utterly defeat the enemy. Fortunately for our fame as soldiers, our enemy is worthy of us. The German is a war-trained veteran—confident, brave, ruthless. We are brave. We are better-equipped, better fed, and in the place of his blood-gutted Woten, we have with us the God of our fathers known of old. The justice of our cause and not the greatness of our race makes us confident. But we are not ruthless, not vicious, not aggressive, therein lies our weakness.

Children of a free and sheltered people who have lived a generous life, we have not the pugnacious disposition of those oppressed beasts our enemies, who must fight or starve. Our bravery is too negative. We talk too much of sacrifice, of the glory of dying that freedom may live. Of course we are willing to die but that is not enough. We must be eager to kill, to inflict on the enemy—the hated enemy—wounds, death and destruction. If we die killing, well and good, but if we fight hard enough, viciously enough, we will kill and live. Live to return to our family and our girl as conquering heroes—men of Mars.

The reputation of our army, the future of our race, your own glory rests in your hands. I know you will be worthy.[31]

One month after the disaster at Kasserine Pass, Patton led the American army at the battle of Gafsa and El Guettar. The night before, March 15, he recorded his thoughts in his diary:

A horrible [day].... Everything there was time to do has been done. Not enough, but all there is time for. Now it is

up to others [to fight] and I have not too much confidence
in any of them. Wish I were triplets and could personally
command two divisions and the corps. Bradley, Gaffey, and
Lambert are a great comfort.

God help me and see to it that I do my duty, but I must
have Your help. I am the best there is, but of myself I am
not enough. "Give us the victory, Lord."

Went to bed and slept well till 0600.

Patton's army was victorious at El Guettar, and the Germans
learned that the United States Army, led by its new commander, was
no longer to be taken lightly.

After the invasion of Sicily, the Protestant Patton began worshipping at Catholic churches, as he explained in a letter to his father-in-
law, Frederick Ayer: "Ever since I got to Sicily I have been going to
Catholic Churches, largely for political reasons but also as a means of
worshipping God because I think he is quite impartial as to the form
in which he is approached."[32]

Many Americans had a hard time reconciling newspaper accounts
of Patton's colorful language and hell-raising style with the traditional
image of a devout Christian. Patton wrote to his wife, "I had a letter...
from a preacher.... He hoped I thought about Jesus and reminded me
that I would die and go to hell if I did not. I wrote him that I was
amazed at his temerity in writing me such a letter when I was a far
better Christian than he was."[33]

He protested his Christian *bona fides* in a letter to Donald M.
Taylor of Peoria, Illinois, dated May 30, 1943:

In spite of the efforts of the newspapers to paint me as a
most profane and ungodly man, I am probably just as
religious as you are. I am a Communicant of the Episcopal
Church and attend services every Sunday.

I have received several letters from people making an earnest effort to save my soul, which, personally, I do not believe is in any grave danger.[34]

Monsignor O'Neill, the Third Army's head chaplain, recognized that profanity was Patton's way of grabbing the attention of his troops. "When the hard-talking commander swore at men lingering on the beaches, he did so because he wanted to be immediately understood, and because he wanted to save men's lives." Patton's aide Lieutenant Colonel Charles Codman insisted that, despite Patton's flair for profanity, "I have never heard the General tell a really sacrilegious or dirty story or encourage the telling of one."[35]

Patton himself relished mixing the sacred and the profane. In August 1944, in the middle of the European campaign, a family friend in Pasadena wrote to him requesting that he be the godfather for their newborn son. Patton replied, "I should certainly consider it a great honor to be little Dick's Godfather. I am sure that he could never find a more God-fearing, God-damning Godfather than myself."[36]

Harry H. Semmes, who served under Patton in both world wars, appreciated the uniqueness of Patton's religious conviction:

From his adolescence, he had always read the Bible, particularly the life of Christ and the wars of the Old Testament. He knew by heart the order of morning prayer of the Episcopal Church. His thoughts, as demonstrated daily to those close to him, repeatedly indicated that his life was dominated by a feeling of dependence on God.... [H]e turned to God for comfort in adversity and to give thanks in success. General Patton was an unusual mixture of a profane and highly religious man.[37]

Coy Eklund recalled Patton's delight in shocking the pious:

> On one occasion I escorted a group of U.S. Congressmen,
> about a dozen of them—including Clare Boothe Luce[38]—
> visiting the war zone. I phoned him [Patton] and then
> escorted them to his house trailer where a cordial visit
> ensued. When Luce noticed a Bible on Patton's camp table
> she asked excitedly, "General, do you read the Bible?"
>
> "Every goddamned day," he replied.[39]

After Patton's army landed in Sicily he attended a private mass in the
chapel of a castle, which he described in a letter to his wife, dated
August 2, 1943:

> The middle part of the castle was built before 1000 and
> there is a chapel in it built by a Norman duke in 1040. The
> old Monsenieur [sic] who runs it told me that it was
> reserved for royalty but insisted on having a mass for me
> so I went all alone. He wanted to make it a Tedium [Te
> Deum] mass, but I insisted on a low one as not knowing the
> rules, I decided to kneel all the time. It was not too bad, as
> I had a royal red velvet priedieu. He is a fine old man and
> hates Mus[solini].
>
> The walls are covered with frescoes and the part back
> of the altar is full of pictures made of inlaid stones. The
> head of Christ is the finest I have ever seen. All conquerors
> have made up to the priests of the conquered....[40]

Mindful of ecclesiastical courtesy, Patton had recently visited the
archbishop of Palermo. He wrote about the meeting in his diary on
July 26:

Called on the Cardinal. He lives in a convent as his palace was bombed. He is very small and quite intelligent. They took a lot of pictures of us in the bosom of the church. I offered to kiss his ring but Keyes[41] said no, that only the faithful did that—he did it. We went into a chapel and prayed. The Mother Superior is a French woman and we talked a little.... I feel that he [the cardinal] is on our side and this fact will have a good effect on the inhabitants.[42]

Patton invited Eisenhower's chauffeur, Kay Summersby, and Ruth Briggs, the secretary of Eisenhower's chief of staff, to visit him in Sicily. He gave them a personal tour that ended at a medieval church near Palermo. After delivering a brief lecture on medieval architecture, Summersby wrote, Patton "sank to his knees and prayed aloud for the success of his troops, for the health and happiness of his family and for a safe flight back for Ruth and me. He was completely unselfconscious."[43]

A former NATO commander, General John R. Galvin, tells the story of a priest who in 1945 came upon Patton in a medieval church in the historic southern German town of Bad Wimpfen am Berg. According to the cleric, "Patton was doing a most unusual thing for a man of such a reputation. The warrior, with notebook and pencil in hand, was calmly sketching the stained-glass windows."[44]

Prayer was a serious undertaking for Patton, who distinguished between his prayers in sport and his prayers in war. When his young daughters saw him on his knees praying before a horse show in which he was competing, they asked if he was praying to win. Patton seemed offended by the question. "That would be insulting to God," he responded. "I just pray to do my best."[45] In war, however, he always asked for victory. Patton required his children to read a verse of the Bible each night and give him their interpretation of it at breakfast.

After listening, he would share with them his own thoughts on the passages they had chosen.[46]

CHAPTER THIRTEEN

SAVING A SOUL

*"I want to tell you officially and definitely that if you are
again guilty of any indiscretion in speech or action...I will
relieve you instantly from command."*

—EISENHOWER IN A LETTER TO PATTON, APRIL 29, 1944

I n April 1944, just two months before the D-Day landings at Normandy, General George S. Patton Jr. was about to be relieved of his command of the Third Army. He was likely to be reduced in rank from general to colonel and then sent home in disgrace. Before meeting with Patton to notify him personally, Eisenhower sent the following cable to the army chief of staff, General George C. Marshall:

I HAVE SENT FOR PATTON TO ALLOW HIM OPPOR-
TUNITY TO PRESENT HIS CASE PERSONALLY TO
ME. ON ALL THE EVIDENCE NOW AVAILABLE I
WILL RELIEVE HIM FROM COMMAND AND SEND
HIM HOME UNLESS SOME NEW AND UNFORESEEN
INFORMATION SHOULD BE DEVELOPED IN THE
CASE.

Omar Bradley agreed with his boss's verdict: "I fully concurred in Ike's decision to send Patton home. I, too, was fed up."[1] The previous day, Eisenhower had already issued a formal letter to Patton severely reprimanding him:

> I have warned you time and again against your impulsiveness... and have flatly instructed you to say nothing that could possibly be misinterpreted.... You first came into my command at my own insistence because I believed in your fighting qualities and your ability to lead troops in battle. At the same time I have always been fully aware of your habit of dramatizing yourself and of committing indiscretions for no other apparent purpose than of calling attention to yourself. I am thoroughly weary of your failure to control your tongue and have begun to doubt your all-around judgment, so essential in high military position. My decision in the present case will not become final until I have heard from the War Department.... I want to tell you officially and definitely that if you are again guilty of any indiscretion in speech or action... I will relieve you instantly from command.[2]

A nervous Patton appeared at Eisenhower's office on the morning of May 1. Patton's opponents, Eisenhower told him, were arguing that even if he was the best tactician and strategist in the army, his demonstrated lack of judgment made him unfit for command. It did not help that it was an election year, added Eisenhower. He told Patton that he had written him a "savage" letter of reprimand and that Washington was forcing his hand. Patton defiantly replied that if he was reduced to the rank of colonel he would demand the right to command one of the assault regiments on D-Day.

After leaving Eisenhower's office, Patton recorded the exchange in his diary, concluding, "My final thought on the matter is that I am destined to achieve some great thing—what I don't know, but this last incident was so trivial in its nature, but so terrible in its effect, that it is not the result of an accident but the work of God. His Will be done."[3]

Patton's salvation came in the form of a cable from General Marshall to Eisenhower:

> THE DECISION IS EXCLUSIVELY YOURS. MY VIEW, AND IT IS MERELY THAT, IS THAT YOU SHOULD NOT WEAKEN YOUR HAND FOR OVERLORD.[4] IF YOU THINK THAT PATTON'S REMOVAL DOES WEAKEN YOUR PROSPECT, YOU SHOULD CONTINUE HIM IN COMMAND. IN ANY EVENT, I DO NOT WANT YOU AT THIS TIME TO BE BURDENED WITH THE RESPONSIBILITY OF REDUCING HIM IN RANK. SEND HIM HOME IF YOU SEE FIT.... CONSIDER ONLY OVERLORD AND YOUR OWN HEAVY BURDEN OF RESPONSIBILITY FOR ITS SUCCESS. EVERYTHING ELSE IS OF MINOR IMPORTANCE.

Marshall's artfully worded cable is a wonderful example of a superior guiding a subordinate to a decision without seeming to undercut his authority. While Marshall makes it clear that responsibility for the decision lies solely with Eisenhower, he mentions his own opinion, almost as if in passing. Marshall knew that the politically savvy and sensitive Eisenhower would give weight to his superior's thoughts no matter how casually they were expressed.

The offense that jeopardized Patton's career was a remark he had made at the opening of the Welcome Club for American GIs in

Knutsford, Eng... ... was a service organization run by l... ...e chairwoman introduced Patton to t... ...mostly local women,
she commented, ...on is not here officially and is speaking
in a purely friendly way." Patton mistakenly assumed that either there
were no reporters present or that his "friendly" remarks were off the
record. Both assumptions were wrong.

His brief remarks were classic Patton, mixing elements of the
profane with political insensitivity, and a clumsy attempt to ingrati-
ate himself with his largely female audience. "[M]y only experience
of welcoming has been to welcome Germans and Italians to the
'Infernal Regions.' In this I have been quite successful," he boasted.
"I feel such clubs as this are a very real value, because I believe with
Mr. Bernard Shaw...that the British and Americans are two people
separated by a common language, and since it is the evident destiny
of the British and Americans, and, of course, the Russians, to rule
the world, the better we know each other, the better job we will do."
Finally, he added that "as soon as our soldiers meet and know the
English ladies and write home and tell our women how truly lovely
you are, the sooner the American ladies will get jealous and force
this war to a quick conclusion, and I will get a chance to go and kill
Japanese."[5]

Patton learned that there had been a reporter present when a story
appeared the next day in British newspapers. Then the story somehow
evaded censors and was picked up by the wire services. When it hit
the United States, it gave the impression that Patton had predicted
that Britain and the United States (and not their Soviet allies) were
destined to rule the post-war world.

Politicians and newspaper editors could not resist the opportunity
to lash out at Patton's suggestion of Anglo-American world domina-
tion. (A chastened Patton was wise enough not to publicly state what

he later told his father-in-law, Fred Ayers—"Anybody, Freddy, who wants the Russians to rule any part of this world is a God-damned fool.") The *Washington Post* took offense at Patton's welcoming his enemies into hell as well as to his references to English and American "dames." The comment, fumed the editors, was "neither gracious nor amusing.... [W]e think that Lieutenant Generals... ought to talk with rather more dignity than this. When they do not they risk losing the respect of the men they command and the confidence of the public they serve. We think this has happened to General Patton. Whatever his merits as a strategist or tactician he has revealed glaring defects as a leader of men." In an unnecessary escalation of the incident, the editorial called on the Senate to disapprove a permanent promotion list that included Patton's name.[6,7]

Karl Mundt, a Republican congressman from South Dakota, complained on the House floor of Patton's slap in "the face of every one of the United Nations, except Great Britain." Mundt's choice of metaphors was deliberate. In a notorious episode the previous November, Patton had slapped a soldier suffering from combat fatigue. Without the earlier scandal, Knutsford probably would not have registered with the press. As Omar Bradley observed, "What would have passed as a local boner coming from anybody less than Patton had promptly exploded into a world crisis."[8]

There had actually been *two* slapping incidents. Patton had been riding a wave of congratulations for his successful invasion and pacification of the island of Sicily. From President Roosevelt: "All of us are thrilled.... My thanks and enthusiastic approbation." British General Harold Alexander: "My sincerest admiration for not only your recent great feat of arms in taking Messina, but for the speed and skill you have shown in the Sicilian operation. Your country will be very proud of you and so am I to have the honor of having under my command such magnificent troops." General George C. Marshall: "You have

done a grand job of leadership and your corps and division commanders and their people have made Americans very proud of their army
and confident of the future."[9]

On August 3, 1943, Patton learned that he was to be awarded the
Distinguished Service Cross for "extraordinary heroism." Later that
day he visited an evacuation hospital outside Nicosia that held many
wounded troops. Coming across Private Charles H. Kuhl, who showed
no visible wounds, Patton asked the soldier why he was there. He was
not wounded, Kuhl replied—"I guess I can't take it." Patton flew into
a rage. He cursed the private, calling him a coward, and ordered him
to leave the tent. When the frightened soldier sat frozen, Patton grew
angrier. He slapped Kuhl's face with a glove, grabbed him by the shirt
collar, and pushed him out of the tent with a final kick in the rear.

Two days later Patton issued the following memo to all of his commanders:

> It has come to my attention that a very small number of
> soldiers are going to the hospital on the pretext that they
> are nervously incapable of combat. Such men are cowards
> and bring discredit on the army and disgrace to their com-
> rades, whom they heartlessly leave to endure the dangers
> of battle while they, themselves, use the hospital as a means
> of escape. You will take measures to see that such cases are
> not sent to the hospital but are dealt with in their units.
> Those who are not willing to fight will be tried by court-
> martial for cowardice in the face of the enemy.

A week later, Patton made an unannounced visit to another evacuation hospital, where he came across Private Paul Bennett, a twenty-
one-year-old who had served in the army for four years. The second
scene was far uglier than the first. Bennett had not had any difficulties
until his buddy was wounded. That night he was unable to sleep and

became increasingly unnerved by the shelling. He was sent to a rear echelon where he was given medicine to make him sleep, but he was still nervous and worried about his wounded friend. The next day a medical officer ordered him evacuated, even though he begged not to be because he wanted to remain with his unit.

When Patton encountered Bennett, the private was huddled up and shivering. Patton asked what his trouble was. "It's my nerves," said Bennett, sobbing.

"What did you say?" screamed Patton.

"It's my nerves, I can't stand the shelling anymore," said Bennett, still sobbing.

"Your nerves, hell; you are just a goddamned coward, you yellow son of a bitch." Patton then slapped Bennett. "Shut up that goddamned crying. I won't have these brave men here who have been shot at seeing a yellow bastard sitting here crying." He then struck the soldier again, knocking his helmet liner off his head and into the next tent. Patton turned to the admitting officer and yelled, "Don't admit this yellow bastard; there's nothing the matter with him. I won't have the hospitals cluttered up with these sons of bitches who haven't got the guts to fight."

Patton then turned back to Bennett, who was shaking, and said, "You're going back to the front lines and you may get shot and killed, but you're going to fight. If you don't, I'll stand you up against a wall and have a firing squad kill you on purpose." Patton then reached for his pistol. "In fact, I ought to shoot you myself, you goddamned whimpering coward." As he left the tent, the general was still yelling back to the receiving officer to "send the yellow son of a bitch back to the front line."

To be fair to Patton, although today the effects of post-traumatic stress disorder are much better understood, what was known in Patton's day as "shell shock" or "combat fatigue" was equated by many with malingering or cowardice. Patton knew that panic and fear were a contagion that could spread through an army like a plague. He was committed to doing everything he could do to stop it.

In addition to the tremendous stress of managing an army in the middle of a war, Patton bore the terrible burden of giving orders that would send thousands of young men to be maimed or killed in combat. About three months before the first slapping incident, Patton wrote in his diary about a visit to the combat ward of a hospital:

Diary, March 23, 1943

The Lord helped a lot today. I visited the Surgical Hospital—it was pretty gruesome but it was strange how the men followed me with their eyes, fearing I would not speak to each one. I talked to all who were conscious. One little boy said, "Are you General Patton?" I said, "Yes," and he said, "Oh, God." Another one said, "You know me. You made a talk to my battalion at Casablanca." I told him I remembered him well.[10]

Patton's daughter Ruth Ellen had a glimpse of that burden soon after the war's end when her father and mother visited Walter Reed Hospital, where she had worked for two years. The Pattons were accompanied by doctors and dignitaries as well as a gaggle of press men. Just before entering the ward, Patton clutched his trademark swagger stick in his gloved left hand, turned to the reporters, and barked, "I'll bet you goddamn buzzards are just following me in here to see if I'll slap another soldier, aren't you? You're hoping I will." As he walked slowly down the long aisle between the white hospital beds in the amputation ward, "all the patients were looking at him with their hearts in their eyes." Patton then returned to the center of the room, wiping away tears, and told the wounded soldiers, "If I had been a better general, most of you would not be here."[11] He then turned on his heel and walked rapidly to the door, with the patients cheering him as he went by.

In her memoir, *The Button Box*, Ruth Ellen recalls a revealing incident that occurred years before World War II. Her father was tutoring her in algebra, and she became recalcitrant:

> It was eleven o'clock, two hours past my bedtime. Georgie was sweating and shouting, and I started to have hysterics for the first and only time in my life. When I suddenly found out that I could not stop crying, I began to enjoy it.... All at once he turned and slapped me so hard that I fell right off my chair. I also stopped having hysterics. He strode out of the room banging the door. Having nothing better to do, I started to go to bed.[12]

Patton's slap seems to have been neither an act of discipline nor an impulsive expression of anger. Though harsh corporal punishment was widely accepted at the time, Ruth Ellen could recall only one other instance when her father had physically disciplined her. In all likelihood, the incident reflected his belief, common at the time, that a slap, clinically administered, was the best way to restore someone from an attack of hysterics. The success of the tactic in this case may have confirmed Patton's belief in its appropriateness.

Several days before exploding at Bennett, Patton had visited another field hospital, where he had seen several horribly injured soldiers. One man was mortally wounded, his head mostly blown off. "He was a horrid bloody mess and not good to look at, or I might develop personal feelings about sending men into battle. That would be fatal for a General."[13] The day before slapping Kuhl, Patton had pinned Purple Hearts on forty wounded soldiers in a hospital, including one dying man who had an oxygen mask over his face. When another soldier told Patton he had been wounded in the chest, Patton would respond, "Well, it may interest you to know the last German I saw had no chest and no head either."[14] Patton later spoke to a group of reporters and presciently remarked: "I do a lot of things people don't give me credit for and I'm not as big a bastard as a lot of people think. The commander of invading troops is under great tension and may do things he later regrets."[15]

Private Kuhl himself offered perhaps the most insightful comment on Patton's psychology at the time of the slapping incidents: "I think he was suffering a little battle fatigue himself."[16] A general who led from the front, Patton frequently exposed himself to artillery fire and shelling. Three days before the second slapping incident, Patton's command post came under long-range German artillery fire. Writing in his diary, Patton admitted that the shelling bothered him and that he was ashamed of himself.[17] Kuhl's own father, a casket maker from Mishawaka, Indiana, wrote to his congressman, forgiving the slap and supporting Patton's promotion.[18]

Patton had experienced combat before World War II, first in 1916 as part of the punitive expedition with Pershing, then in the trenches of the First World War. While commanding a tank crew, he had occasion to test his courage. A defective round exploded in the muzzle of the tanks' cannon, injuring several soldiers. The next round exploded in the breech and blew off the gunner's head. The men were reluctant to fire the next round, Patton recalled, so to restore their confidence he fired the cannon himself three times. "I have never in my life been more reluctant to pull a trigger," he admitted.[19]

On another occasion, Patton walked along the American line to inspire his troops and test his own mettle under fire. He felt satisfied with his own display of gallantry until he noticed a figure standing atop a small hill even more exposed than he was. It was Douglas MacArthur, then a thirty-eight-year-old brigadier general. Patton joined him on the hilltop as German artillery crept up on their position. Little conversation was exchanged as the shelling continued. Patton later wrote, "Each one [of us] wanted to leave but each hated to say so, so we let it come over us."[20] MacArthur's biographer writes that "Patton flinched at one point and then looked annoyed with himself, whereupon the brigadier said dryly, 'Don't worry, Major [sic]; you never hear the one that gets you.'"[21]

The terror of the day he was wounded at Cheppy and his war experience left their mark on Patton after he returned from World War I in March 1919. During Prohibition, he stored bottles of home-made beer in the covered walkway to the kitchen shack. One night, hearing a series of short explosions like machine gun fire, Patton dropped to the floor, to the amazement of his family. The cook screamed from the kitchen that the homemade brew was exploding. Patton arose red-faced and explained that the noise had reminded him of being under fire during the war. Beatrice laughed and called him her "hero" before the horror on her husband's face registered with her. Then she fully appreciated the trauma that he had experienced during the war.[22]

Reporters from the *Saturday Evening Post, Newsweek,* NBC, and CBS eventually learned about the slapping incidents. Exercising restraint that is unimaginable today, the reporters made no attempt to file the story but brought it directly to Eisenhower's attention. Demaree Bess of the *Saturday Evening Post* delivered a written summary to Eisenhower's chief of staff, Bedell Smith. The report noted that striking an enlisted man was a court-martial offense. The reporters were unaware that Eisenhower had received a report on the incident from army medical personnel two days earlier. While disturbed by the initial report, Ike was inclined to believe that it might be exaggerated, and he intended to discipline Patton privately.

Eisenhower then met with the reporters, who proposed a deal: they would kill the story, but in return they wanted Patton fired. The meeting revealed the strong anti-Patton feeling among the press. One of the reporters told Eisenhower that there were "at least 50,000 American soldiers in Sicily who would shoot Patton if they had a chance." Another said he thought Patton had gone temporarily insane.

Eisenhower refused the blackmail. Instead he condemned Patton's actions, explaining that he had already written him a letter of reprimand that ordered him to apologize personally for his behavior. Then in a scene that could occur only in the strongest democracy in the world, the Supreme Allied Commander in Europe felt compelled to justify to three reporters why he was keeping one of his generals, despite their personal objections:

> His emotional tenseness and his impulsiveness are the very qualities that make him, in open situations, such a remarkable leader of an Army.... In pursuit and exploitation there is need for a commander who sees nothing but the necessity of getting ahead. The more he drives his men the more he saves their lives. He must be indifferent to fatigue and ruthless in demanding the last atom of physical energy. Patton is such a commander. I feel, therefore, that Patton should be saved for the great battles facing us in Europe.

Eisenhower said he would not censor their reports if they chose to write of the incident, but he explained that the incident would be of propaganda value to the enemy and embarrass the United States Army command. This gentleman's agreement between Eisenhower and the reporters successfully suppressed the story for three months, even though it continued to be widely discussed within the army.

Eventually, however, the Washington columnist Drew Pearson, not a war correspondent and therefore not subject to army censorship, learned of the story. Pearson submitted his story to domestic censors who contacted the War Department, which urged that the story be killed because of its feared effect on morale. The domestic censors felt that these grounds were too tenuous to bar the story, and they gave Pearson approval to run it.[23]

On November 21, 1943, Pearson let his nationwide radio audience in on a "secret" that was widely known among American war correspondents and thousands of U.S. soldiers—for slapping a hospitalized soldier, Patton had been "severely reprimanded" by General Eisenhower. The next day, however, a spokesman for Allied Headquarters in Algiers issued a misleading communiqué: "General Patton has never been reprimanded at any time by General Eisenhower." The denial was true only in a highly technical sense. In army protocol, a reprimand is "an official rebuke administered as a punishment" according to strictly defined rules of disciplinary procedure. A written communication informs the officer in question of the charges against him; the accused must acknowledge receipt of the communication and indorse it, and he may demand a trial if he wishes. But the statement was obviously issued knowing that it would be understood to mean that Patton had not been disciplined at all.

Eisenhower was at first unaware that his headquarters had issued a denial, but as soon as he learned of it, he insisted that the record be corrected. The following day, on November 23, an officer admitted that he was "a little ashamed" that what he told the American people was "not the complete truth."[24]

One of the best-known journalists in the country, Pearson was a pioneer of a new muckraking style that focused on exposés of the financial or personal improprieties of public figures. Two of Pearson's employees were themselves eventually exposed as having worked for communist organizations. David Karr, Pearson's chief aide, had worked for two years at the communist newspaper the *Daily Worker*. Years later, declassified FBI files from the VENONA project revealed that Karr was a source for the Soviet secret police and the KGB. Andrew Older, another member of Pearson's staff, was identified in 1951 as member of the Communist Party.[25]

Pearson's radio broadcast regarding the slapping incidents provoked an outcry from newspapers, politicians, and citizens, many of them parents of soldiers serving overseas. Many newspaper editors called for Patton's resignation. Representative Jed Johnson of Oklahoma wrote to the army chief of staff, George C. Marshall, calling Patton's actions "despicable" and saying he was "amazed and chagrined" that Patton was still commanding the Seventh Army.[26] On the floor of the House, Representative Charles B. Hoeven of Iowa complained that parents of "boys in the service" had no need of additional anxiety and worry over whether "hard-boiled officers" were abusing their sons.[27]

After each of the slapping incidents, Patton had said to the officers with him that he had probably just "saved an immortal soul."[28] He used the same phrase in a statement of November 27, 1943, that he prepared for secretary of war, Henry Stimson:[29]

> This letter is not intended as an excuse for obvious mistakes or as a plea for sympathy.
>
> I believe that in war the good of the individual must be subordinated to the good of the army.
>
> I have never asked favors or immunity for myself, and I have never granted them to those serving under me. I have, to the best of my ability, undergone all the risks of my troops.
>
> I love and admire good soldiers and brave men. I hate and despise slackers and cowards.
>
> I am quite tender-hearted and emotional in my dealings with wounded men.
>
> Like all commanders I am constantly faced with the problem of malingering. If it is not checked, it spreads like prairie fire....
>
> I inspected some 300 freshly wounded men who had gallantly and unflinchingly done their duty, and who, in spite of their wounds, were cheerful and uncomplaining.

The last man I came to was a forlorn individual sitting on a box, apparently waiting to have a wound dressed. I asked him where he had been hit. He replied that he had not been hit but that he "just could not take it," and had come to the hospital to avoid combat.

The contrast between this cur, who was not only skulking himself but by his cowardice was forcing other loyal and brave men to do his duty, and the heroes I had just been talking to so moved me that I slapped him across the face with the gloves I was carrying in my hand, shook him, and called him a coward, and told him to get back to his outfit and try to be a man.

When I left, I told the officer who was with me that I hoped I had made a man of that thing, and that if so, I had saved an immortal soul.

The other practically identical incident….

I had just talked to over a hundred wounded, the last of whom had lost his right arm and was joking about it, when I came on a second of these human jackals, who also told me "He could not take it." I simply shook him, cussed him out, and told the hospital to return him to his outfit.

There is no doubt that my method was too forthright. They will not be repeated.

General Eisenhower wrote me a forceful personal letter very rightly calling my attention to the bad effects my action had on public opinion and directing me to make certain amends.

I apologized to the two men. I called in the medical personnel who witnessed the incidents, explaining to them the reasons for my action, and my regret for same. I made a speech to each of the divisions telling the men what great soldiers they were, explaining to them what they were fighting for, and emphasizing how proud I was of them. I ended by saying that if any of them felt I had been too severe, I apologized, but for every man I had corrected for his own good, I had complimented a thousand.

Any other prejudicial statements concerning me as an officer or soldier are not true.

When he wrote about the day he was wounded in World War I, a day when he too had been gripped by fear, Patton alluded to a verse from St. Paul's first letter to the Corinthians, "The last enemy that shall be destroyed is fear of death."[30] To Patton, conquering one's fear was the path to eternal salvation.

Patton was never seduced by technology or new weapons. Wars were won, he believed, by men who were inspired by God to be courageous:

> New weapons are useful in that they add to the repertoire of killing, but, be they tanks or tomahawks, weapons are only weapons after all. Wars are fought with weapons, but they are won by men.... It was the spirit of the Lord, courage, that came mightily upon Samson at Lehi which gained victory—not the jawbone of an ass.[31]

Throughout the tempest in the press, Patton was sustained by his faith in God. In his diary he lamented, "If the fate of the only successful general in this war depends on the statement of a discredited writer like Drew Pearson, we are in a bad lot. Of course, I am worried, but I am quite confident that the Lord will see me through.... I am perfectly certain that this is not the end of me."[32] Nevertheless, he was capable of occasional, if uncharacteristic, self-pity, as his diary reveals:

November 25, 1943

Thanksgiving Day. I had nothing to be thankful for so I did not give thanks.[33]

As he always did during times of trouble, Patton turned to the Bible for solace. Three days after that unthankful Thanksgiving, he recorded:

Naturally I am worried but I am really more angry than uneasy. My side is not being shown and my friends must be having a hell of a time. So far as I can see, there is nothing for me to do except read the Bible and trust to destiny. I certainly do not intend to read any of the dirt published in the papers or broadcast over the radio. There is no use in giving myself indigestion for nothing.[34]

While Patton's commanders were deciding his fate, the allied leaders—Roosevelt, Churchill, and Stalin—met in Tehran to discuss strategy for defeating Germany and plans for the postwar world. Uncertain of the role, if any, he might play in the coming invasion of Europe, Patton took a sightseeing trip to the Holy Land and Malta.[35]

December 14, 1943

We took off by plane for Jerusalem at 0700 and crossed the canal just south of Lake Tenes, which is near where the children of Israel crossed.

It never occurred to me until this flight that, at the time the Jews crossed, it was unnecessary for them to ford anything, because there is a stretch of desert from Bitter Lake to the Mediterranean which had no water on it. However, they did get across and Napoleon crossed at about the same place and also lost his baggage when the wind shifted.

From the canal we flew along the line of Allenby's advance and crossed at Wadi El Arish at the spot where the battle occurred. It is a much less formidable obstacle than I had gathered from the books.

Beersheba and the surrounding country do not look too difficult, but certainly away from the wells the country is an absolute sand sea, and it is difficult to understand how Allenby ever moved a cavalry corps across it.

From Beersheba we flew over Hebron and Bethlehem and turned westward just south of Jerusalem, finally landing at Aqir, near the coast, where we were met with some cars and driven thirty miles to Jerusalem.

The only reason for calling Palestine a "land of milk and honey" is by comparison with the desert immediately surrounding it. It consists of nothing but barren stony hills on which a few olive trees eke out a precarious existence. We did not see a single beehive, although there were quite a number of mimosa trees.

On reaching Jerusalem, we were met by Major General D. F. McConnell, who commands the district. He gave us a British priest, who had lived a long time in Jerusalem, as a guide to see the sights.

We entered the city through the gate which Tancred stormed when the city was first taken (A.D. 1099). The Church of the Holy Sepulchre covers both the Tomb of Christ and also the place where the Cross stood. It is run by a composite group consisting of Catholics, Greeks, and Copts, and by a strange freak of chance, or British political insight, the doorkeeper is a Mohammedan.

It struck me as an anomaly that, during my entire visit to Jerusalem, I was guarded by four secret service men, and the oddest part of it was that, when I entered the Tomb, the secret service men came in with me. People must have very little confidence to fear assassination in such a place.

From the Tomb we went to the Crusaders' Chapel where those who became Knights of Jerusalem were knighted. In this chapel is the sword which is supposed to have been used on these occasions. In my opinion it is a fake, since the pommel is not of the correct shape, nor has it sufficient weight. The pommels of Crusaders' swords were usually carved in the form of a stone or a piece of lead, which in an earlier date had actually been tied there. This pommel was in the shape of a blunt acorn. The crossguard and the shape of the blade were correct.

From here we went to the place where the Cross had stood. Most of the mountain was cut away during the Roman occupation, when they filled up the Tomb and erected a Temple of Venus over both the Mount and the Tomb. However, there is an altar which is supposed to be on the exact spot where the Cross was erected.

While I was in this chapel, I secured a rosary for Mary Scally [his childhood nurse] and had it blessed at the altar.

After we had left the church, we followed the Way of the Cross, which is a dirty street, to the point where the Roman Forum had stood. I should think the distance is less than half a mile. In addition to the Stations of the Cross used by the Catholics, the Greeks have a number of extra ones, so that it is practically a day's trip for a Greek priest to walk down the street, as they have to stop in front of each station.

From the Forum we got into the cars and drove to the Garden of Gethsemane, where there are still olive trees which just possibly may have been in existence at the time of the Crucifixion.

After lunching with the Commanding General, we drove back to the airfield and flew back to Cairo along the coast, passing over Gaza. Although I looked very carefully, I could see no indication of the fighting, but I did recognize the cactus hedge where the tanks got stuck. We reached Cairo just at dark, having completed in one day the trip which took the Children of Israel forty years to accomplish.

After the Holy Land, Patton headed to the Mediterranean island of Malta.[36] He recorded his thoughts in his journal:

Malta, which we reached at three o'clock, is quite different from the way I had pictured it. It is almost completely covered with villages and the areas between them are crowded with tiny fields. The only place where this crowding does not exist is on the airfields....

The most interesting thing I saw is the library of the Knights of Malta. We were taken through this by the librarian. He speaks and reads in script nine languages, so he is perfectly capable of translating the valuable collection of manuscripts in the library.

One codex dating from 1420 and depicting the life of Saint Anthony, who spent his time being pursued by devils in the form of beautiful women, was particularly interesting to me because in one of the pictures it showed an armorer's shop in which suits of armor, varying in date from early 1100 to 1400, were hung up for sale just as one hangs up clothes in a pawnshop. The point of interest is that most historians are prone to classify armor by dates, whereas here we have visual proof that as late as 1400 all types of armor, both mail and plate, were still being used.

Another codex which was interesting was one of the original printings of the Bible, using wood type. In this case all the capitals were omitted and subsequently illuminated by hand.

In order to be a Knight of Malta, it was necessary to have sixteen crosses of nobility, so that when anyone came up to be a knight, he had to present his genealogy, which was then studied by a college of heralds, and, if proven correct, permitted to join. Since all these genealogies, covering the knights from sometime in 1100 to date, are preserved in the library, it gives the greatest historical family tree in the world.

In addition to the requirement of sixteen crosses of nobility, a knight had to spend eighteen months at sea on the galleys as a fighter, and then work in a hospital.

The knights also had to take four vows—Poverty, Chastity, Humility, and Obedience. The vow of Poverty required him to give four-fifths of his then estate to the Order. However, if he was a successful knight, he received from the Order more than a hundredfold over what he gave, so that most of them died very rich. This was particularly true before 1800, when the knights had a sort of stranglehold on the privateering business in the Mediterranean and used their hatred for the Turks as a means of veiling their personally conducted piracy against Turks and against anyone else whom they could catch.

The vow of Chastity was not enforced except by one Grand Master, who, in order to discourage the amorous activities of his dependents, required that all the girls live across the harbor from the forts, so that when a knight wanted to see his lady-love, he had to row across and thereby bring great discredit upon himself. Apparently the discredit consisted of other knights cheering him on.

The vow of Humility was got around by the simple expedient of washing a poor man's feet three times. The vow of Obedience was rigidly enforced.

Patton always looked for signs that he was still in God's favor, especially in times of trouble, and during the firestorm over the slapping incidents, he received it in the form of German artillery shells. In a letter to his wife dated January 11, 1944, Patton described how two German shells had recently struck the spot where he would have been standing had he not stopped to take a picture. Another shell struck where he had been standing while taking the picture. And half the nose of a shell landed about nine inches from his toe, but the shell was already spent. He was exhilarated by the incident, believing that it was a divine sign that he had been spared for something important.

Patton cheerfully explained to his wife, "Mathematically I should be dead as none of the four craters was more than 30 feet from me, but I am not dead or even hurt. It gave me great self confidence. The Lord had a perfect cut for me and pulled his punch."

The next day he reiterated the point in another letter to Beatrice. "You have no idea how much that near miss... cheered me up. I know I am needed!" He also wrote that "Rabbi B. R. Brickner spent an hour with me just now and was much impressed with my prayer.... Well some day I will know what I am to do."[37]

Like the rest of the world, Patton learned of the Normandy invasion by listening to the BBC at seven o'clock on the morning of June

6, 1944.[38] Though he had been sidelined from the invasion, he played an important role in it by his absence. In February 1944, Overlord planners at Supreme Allied Headquarters had formulated a plan— "Operation Fortitude South"—to deceive the Nazi commanders into thinking that the Norman landings were merely a feint to draw German defenders away from a main Allied invasion at Pas de Calais. The Germans were fed information that when the bridgehead was established by six Allied assault divisions, a huge force of fifty divisions would exploit the opening. As the official British history notes, it was "the most complex and successful deception operation in the entire history of the war."[39]

A month after the Normandy invasion, secretly landing at an airstrip near Omaha Beach, Patton entered a waiting jeep. When army and navy personnel rushed up to see him, Patton stood and delivered a short impromptu speech: "I'm proud to be here to fight beside you. Now let's cut the guts out of those Krauts and get the hell on to Berlin. And when we get to Berlin, I am going to personally shoot that paper-hanging goddamned son of a bitch just like I would a snake."

The troops cheered Patton's remarks.[40] He soon learned that he was to lead the Third Army and that his first responsibility was to clear the Brest peninsula of Germans. Patton's presence was still a secret to the enemy. He wrote to Beatrice on July 10, 1944, "Sunday I went to a field mass. It was quite impressive. All the men with rifles and helmets, the altar the back of a jeep. Planes on combat missions flying over and the sound of guns all the while.... There is nothing to do at the moment but be a secret weapon."[41]

Eisenhower prepared to leak a story that Patton had lost his command because of "displeasure at some of his indiscretions" and that the main invasion of the continent was delayed by bad weather. This deception caused the Germans to delay a counter-attack that might have crushed or seriously set back the Allied invasion. By providing a plausible reason for Patton's removal, the notorious slapping incidents contributed to the success of the deception. It is thus one of history's ironies that General Patton's greatest victory might have come in a battle in which he played no active role.

CHAPTER FOURTEEN

PATTON'S PRAYER

"This is General Patton; do you have a good prayer for weather?"

—PATTON IN A CALL TO THE CHAPLAIN
OF THE THIRD ARMY, JOHN H. O'NEILL

On October 22, 1944, Patton met with his commander, General Omar Bradley, and Bradley's chief of staff to discuss plans for taking the French city of Metz and then pushing east into the Saar River Valley, a center of Germany's armaments industry. Bradley, believing that a strong push might well end the war, argued for a simultaneous attack by all of the Allied armies in Europe.

Patton pointed out that there was not enough ammunition, food, or gasoline to support all the armies. There were enough supplies, however, for one army. Patton's Third Army could attack twenty-four hours after getting the signal. After a vigorous debate, Bradley conceded. Patton was told that the attack could take place any time after November 5, and that aerial bombardment would be available beforehand.

The Allies were really fighting three enemies, Patton told Bradley—the Germans, time, and the weather. The weather was the most serious threat. The Third Army's sick rate equaled its battle casualty rate. Patton was never one to delay an attack, convinced that each day's delay gave the enemy more time to prepare. "The best is the enemy of the good" was one of his favorite maxims. It would be better to attack as soon as Bradley could provide him with supplies.

But Patton could not control the weather, which affected weapons, aircraft, and the movement of troops. A student of history, Patton was keenly aware of weather's role in a major operation or campaign. When Kublai Khan attacked the Japanese island of Kyushu with his fleet of forty-four hundred ships in 1281, he encountered a typhoon that destroyed half his fleet. The Japanese saw the storm as a divine wind sent by the gods to save them. In his invasion of Russia in 1812, Napoleon was unprepared for Russia's brutal climate, and thousands of his soldiers perished in the severe winter. He lost more men to cold, famine, and disease than to Russian bullets. Napoleon's defeat confirmed Emperor Nicholas I's dictum that Russia has two generals in which she can confide: Generals January and February.

But Patton could look to more recent lessons about weather and battle. Only four months earlier the fate of the Allied invasion of Europe hung on the course of a storm in the English Channel. A break in the weather on June 6 allowed the amphibious assault on Normandy to proceed. Two weeks later, one of the most severe storms ever to strike Normandy sank or disabled a number of Allied ships and wiped out the American Mulberry artificial harbor off Omaha Beach. The Allied war effort was virtually shut down for five days.[1]

When Patton had completed all his preparations for battle, he turned to the Bible and entrusted everything, including the weather, to God. His diary entry for November 7, 1944, reads:

Two years ago today we were on the *Augusta* approaching Africa, and it was blowing hard. Then about 1600 it stopped. It is now 0230 and raining hard. I hope that too stops.

Know of nothing more I can do to prepare for this attack except to read the Bible and pray. The damn clock seems to have stopped. I am sure we will have great success.

At 1900, Eddy and Grow came to the house to beg me to call off the attack due to the bad weather, heavy rains, and swollen rivers. I told them the attack would go on. I am sure it will succeed. On November 7, 1942, there was a storm but it stopped at 1600. All day the 9th of July 1943, there was a storm but it cleared at dark.

I know the Lord will help us again. Either He will give us good weather or the bad weather will hurt the Germans more than it does us. His Will Be Done.[2]

The Saar campaign was launched on November 8, 1944. After one month's fighting, Patton's Third Army had liberated 873 towns and 1,600 square miles. In addition, they had killed or wounded an estimated 88,000 enemy soldiers and taken another 30,000 prisoner. Patton next prepared for the breakthrough to the River Rhine, a formidable natural obstacle to the invasion of Germany by the Allies. The attack was set for December 19.

In early December 1944, the headquarters of the Third Army was in the Caserne Molifor, an old French military barracks in Nancy in the region of Lorraine, a ninety-minute train ride from Paris. At eleven o'clock on the morning of December 8, Patton telephoned the head chaplain, Monsignor James H. O'Neill: "This is General Patton; do you have a good prayer for weather? We must do something about those rains if we are to win the war."

The taciturn priest was the solid Midwestern type. His rimless round glasses framed his round head and solid jaw, giving him a bookish, intellectual look. The son of an Irish barrel maker, with a mother from Wisconsin, O'Neill was raised in the shadow of the Chicago stockyards in a family of seven children. He was educated by Jesuits at St. Ignatius high school, and after becoming a priest he taught briefly at Carroll College in Helena, Montana. An older brother's appointment to West Point (class of 1911) had sparked the future priest's interest in the military. Initially his bishop resisted releasing O'Neill to serve as a chaplain in the military, but his persistence eventually paid off. Organization was almost as much a religion for O'Neill as his Catholicism. He was thoughtful, a capable administrator, and a man of sincere humility.

There are three competing accounts of what happened after Patton's telephone call to O'Neill. The account of Colonel Paul Harkins, Patton's deputy chief of staff, appears as a footnote in *War As I Knew It*, a book based on Patton's diaries and published in 1947, after his death. Harkin helped to edit the book and wrote this lengthy footnote:

> On or about the fourteenth of December, 1944, General Patton called Chaplain O'Neill, Third Army Chaplain, and myself into his office in Third Headquarters at Nancy. The conversation went something like this:
>
> *General Patton*: "Chaplain, I want you to publish a prayer for good weather. I'm tired of these soldiers having to fight mud and floods as well as Germans. See if we can't get God to work on our side."
>
> *Chaplain O'Neill*: "Sir, it's going to take a pretty thick rug for that kind of praying."

General Patton: "I don't care if it takes a flying carpet. I want the praying done."

Chaplain O'Neill: "Yes, sir. May I say, General, that it usually isn't a customary thing among men of my profession to pray for clear weather to kill fellow men."

General Patton: "Chaplain, are you trying to teach me theology or are you the Chaplain of the Third Army? I want a prayer."

Chaplain O'Neill: "Yes, sir."

Outside, the Chaplain said, "Whew, that's a tough one! What do you think he wants?" It was perfectly clear to me. The General wanted a prayer—he wanted one right now—and he wanted it published to the Command.

The Army Engineer was called in, and we finally decided that our field topographical company could print the prayer on a small-sized card, making enough copies for distribution to the army. It being near Christmas, we also asked General Patton to include a Christmas greeting to the troops on the same card with the prayer. The General agreed, wrote a short greeting, and the card was made up, published, and distributed to the troops on the twenty-second of December.

The year after the publication of *War As I Knew It*, Monsignor O'Neill felt compelled to write his own account of the prayer's origin, which was published in *The Military Chaplain* magazine as "The True Story of the Patton Prayer." O'Neill complained that "the footnote on the Prayer by Colonel Paul D. Harkins.... while containing the elements of a funny story about the General and his Chaplain, is not the true account of the prayer incident or its sequence."

O'Neill maintains that he told Patton over the telephone that he would research the topic and report back to him within an hour. After hanging up, O'Neill looked out at the immoderate rains that had plagued the Third Army's operations for the past three months. As he searched through his prayer books, O'Neill could find no formal prayers pertaining to weather, so he composed an original prayer which he typed on a three-by-five-inch card:

> Almighty and most merciful Father, we humbly beseech Thee, of Thy great goodness, to restrain these immoderate rains with which we have had to contend. Grant us fair weather for Battle. Graciously hearken to us as soldiers who call upon Thee that, armed with Thy power, we may advance from victory to victory, and crush the oppression and wickedness of our enemies and establish Thy justice among men and nations.

Assuming that the prayer was not for Patton's private devotion but for distribution to the troops, O'Neill then decided to draft a Christmas greeting:

> To each officer and soldier in the Third United States Army, I Wish a Merry Christmas. I have full confidence in your courage, devotion to duty, and skill in battle. We march in our might to complete victory. May God's blessings rest upon each of you on this Christmas Day. G. S. Patton, Jr, Lieutenant General, Commanding, Third United States Army.

O'Neill then threw on his trench coat and crossed the quadrangle to Patton's office. Patton read the prayer, returned it to O'Neill, and casually directed the chaplain to "have 250,000 copies printed, and see to it that every man in the Third Army gets one." O'Neill then directed Patton's attention to the Christmas greeting on the reverse side of the card. "Very good," said Patton, with an approving smile.

"If the general would sign the card, it would add a personal touch that I am sure the men would like," said the chaplain. So Patton sat down at his desk, signed the card, and returned it to O'Neill.

The general then continued, "Chaplain, sit down for a moment. I want to talk to you about this business of prayer." Patton rubbed his face in his hands, sat silently for a moment, then rose up and walked to the high window of the office where he stood with his back to O'Neill, watching the falling rain. O'Neill later recalled,

> As usual, he was dressed stunningly, and his six-foot-two powerfully built physique made an unforgettable silhouette against the great window. The General Patton I saw there was the Army Commander to whom the welfare of the men under him was a matter of personal responsibility. Even in the heat of combat he could take time out to direct new methods to prevent trench feet, to see to it that dry socks went forward daily with the rations to troops on the line, to kneel in the mud administering morphine and caring for a wounded soldier until the ambulance came. What was coming now?
>
> "Chaplain, how much praying is being done in the Third Army?" inquired the general.
>
> "Does the general mean by chaplains, or by the men?" asked O'Neill.
>
> "By everybody," Patton replied.
>
> "I am afraid to admit it, but I do not believe that much praying is going on. When there is fighting, everyone prays, but now with this constant rain—when things are quiet, dangerously quiet, men just sit and wait for things to happen. Prayer out here is difficult. Both chaplains and men are removed from a special building with a steeple. Prayer to most of them is a formal, ritualized affair, involving

special posture and a liturgical setting. I do not believe that much praying is being done."

Patton left the window, sat at his desk and leaned back in his swivel chair. Playing with a pencil, he began to speak again.

"Chaplain, I am a strong believer in Prayer. There are three ways that men get what they want; by planning, by working, and by Praying. Any great military operation takes careful planning, or thinking. Then you must have well-trained troops to carry it out: that's working. But between the plan and the operation there is always an unknown. That unknown spells defeat or victory, success or failure. It is the reaction of the actors to the ordeal when it actually comes. Some people call that getting the breaks; I call it God. God has His part, or margin, in everything. That's where prayer comes in. Up to now, in the Third Army, God has been very good to us. We have never retreated; we have suffered no defeats, no famine, no epidemics. This is because a lot of people back home are praying for us. We were lucky in Africa, in Sicily, and in Italy. Simply because people prayed. But we have to pray for ourselves, too. A good soldier is not made merely by making him think and work. There is something in every soldier that goes deeper than thinking or working—it's his 'guts.' It is something that he has built in there: it is a world of truth and power that is higher than himself. Great living is not all output of thought and work. A man has to have intake as well. I don't know what you call it, but I call it religion, prayer, or God."

O'Neill continues,

He talked about Gideon in the Bible, said that men should pray no matter where they were, in church or out of it, that if they did not pray, sooner or later they would "crack up." To all this I commented agreement, that one of the major training objectives of my office was to help soldiers recover and make their lives effective in this third realm, prayer. It would do no harm to re-impress this training on chaplains. We had about 486 chaplains in the Third Army at that time, representing 32 denominations. Once the Third Army had become operational, my mode of contact with the chaplains had been chiefly through Training Letters issued from time to time to the Chaplains in the four corps and the 22 to 26 divisions comprising the Third Army. Each treated of a variety of subjects of corrective or training value to a chaplain working with troops in the field.

"I wish," said Patton, "you would put out a Training Letter on this subject of Prayer to all the chaplains; write about nothing else, just the importance of prayer. Let me see it before you send it. We've got to get not only the chaplains but every man in the Third Army to pray. We must ask God to stop these rains. These rains are that margin that holds defeat or victory. If we all pray, it will be like what Dr. Carrel said, it will be like plugging in on a current whose source is in Heaven. I believe that prayer completes that circuit. It is power."

With that the general rose from his chair, indicating that the meeting was concluded, and O'Neill returned to his office to prepare the training letter Patton had requested.

The "Dr. Carrel" to whom Patton referred was Alexis Carrel, a French surgeon and biologist. Carrel was awarded the Nobel Prize for medicine in 1912 and appeared twice on the cover of *Time*. He has been credited with having initiated all major advances in modern surgery, including organ transplants.³ Carrel was perhaps the most famous doctor in the world. Many were captivated by Carrel's attempts to keep organs alive indefinitely outside the body. One of those fascinated by Carrel's experiments was the American aviator Charles Lindbergh, who enjoyed a long collaboration with Carrel's scientific projects.

Although he had been raised Catholic, Carrel became the epitome of the skeptical, rational-minded scientist. Describing himself in the third person, he wrote:

> Absorbed in his scientific studies his mind had been strongly attracted to the German system of critical analysis and he had slowly become convinced that outside of the positivist method no certainties existed. His religious ideas, ground down by the analytic process, had finally been destroyed, leaving him only a lovely memory of a delicate and beautiful dream.
>
> He then had taken refuge in tolerant skepticism. He had horror of all that was sectarian; he was prepared to acknowledge the value of any sincere belief.⁴

Carrel became fascinated with the power of prayer, however, following a trip in 1902 to Lourdes, where he witnessed the miraculous cure of a young woman named Marie Bailly. Her condition was so grave that Carrel did not believe she would survive the train ride to Lourdes. He wrote:

> There is one patient who is closer to death at this moment than any of the others. I have already been called to her bedside several times.... This unfortunate girl is in the last stages of tubercular peritonitis. I know her history. Her

whole family died of tuberculosis. She has had tubercular sores, lesions of the lungs, and now for the last few months a peritonitis diagnosed both by a general practitioner and by the well-known Bordeaux surgeon, Bromillax. Her condition is very grave; I had to give her morphine on the journey. She may die at any moment right under my nose. If such a case as hers were cured, it would indeed be a miracle. I would never doubt again; I would become a monk!

Arriving at the baths adjoining the grotto at Lourdes, Marie asked that the water be poured on her abdomen. Three times this was done. The first time, Marie told of a searing pain all over her body. The second time, she felt much less pain, and when the water was poured on her the third time, it gave her a very pleasant sensation. Carrel carefully witnessed the proceedings, recording the time, pulse, facial expressions, and any other details he could. Within thirty minutes, the young woman's abdomen, which had been enormously distended and very hard, had flattened and any distortions had completely disappeared. No discharge was ever observed from the body.[5]

Carrel was stunned. He had a psychiatrist test Marie every two weeks for four months. She was regularly tested for traces of tuberculosis as well. By late November she was declared to be in good health both physically and mentally, and the next month she entered the novitiate in Paris where she lived the arduous life of a Sister of Charity. She died in 1937 at the age of fifty-eight having never had a relapse.[6]

Carrel struggled to explain what he had witnessed. He knew that the medical science of the time could not explain Marie Bailly's recovery. He began to study the phenomena of prayer and miraculous cures but did so secretly, fearful that if his interest were discovered it would be "dangerous to his career." Ever the skeptic, Carrel was reluctant to credit the miracle to God's work but would forever be fascinated with the power of prayer as a psychic force.

Carrel died on November 5, 1944, a month before O'Neill's meeting with Patton on the topic of prayer. Patton's reference to Carrel was almost certainly prompted by obituaries of the world's most famous doctor. O'Neill recalled a story in the press in which Carrel described prayer "as one of the most powerful forms of energy that man can generate."

The day after O'Neill had shown Patton the prayer for fair weather for battle and the accompanying Christmas greeting, he presented the general with Training Letter No. 5. Patton read it and directed that it be circulated without change to all of the Third Army's 486 chaplains, as well as to every organization commander down to and including the regimental level. In total, 3,200 copies were distributed over O'Neill's signature to every unit in the Third Army. As the chaplain noted, however, strictly speaking it was the Third Army commander's letter, not O'Neill's. The order came directly from Patton himself. Distribution was completed on December 11 and 12.

> TRAINING LETTER NO. 5
>
> December 14, 1944
>
> Chaplains of the Third Army:
>
> At this stage of the operations I would call upon the chaplains and the men of the Third United States Army to focus their attention on the importance of prayer.
>
> Our glorious march from the Normandy Beach across France to where we stand, before and beyond the Siegfried Line, with the wreckage of the German Army behind us should convince the most skeptical soldier that God has ridden with our banner. Pestilence and famine have not touched us. We have continued in unity of purpose. We have had no quitters; and our leadership has been masterful. The Third Army has no roster of Retreats. None of

Defeats. We have no memory of a lost battle to hand on to our children from this great campaign.

But we are not stopping at the Siegfried Line. Tough days may be ahead of us before we eat our rations in the Chancellery of the Deutsches Reich.

As chaplains it is our business to pray. We preach its importance. We urge its practice. But the time is now to intensify our faith in prayer, not alone with ourselves, but with every believing man, Protestant, Catholic, Jew, or Christian in the ranks of the Third United States Army.

Those who pray do more for the world than those who fight; and if the world goes from bad to worse, it is because there are more battles than prayers. "Hands lifted up," said Bossuet, "smash more battalions than hands that strike." Gideon of Bible fame was least in his father's house. He came from Israel's smallest tribe. But he was a mighty man of valor. His strength lay not in his military might, but in his recognition of God's proper claims upon his life. He reduced his Army from thirty-two thousand to three hundred men lest the people of Israel would think that their valor had saved them. We have no intention to reduce our vast striking force. But we must urge, instruct, and indoctrinate every fighting man to pray as well as fight. In Gideon's day, and in our own, spiritually alert minorities carry the burdens and bring the victories.

Urge all of your men to pray, not alone in church, but everywhere. Pray when driving. Pray when fighting. Pray alone. Pray with others. Pray by night and pray by day. Pray for the cessation of immoderate rains, for good weather for Battle. Pray for the defeat of our wicked enemy whose banner is injustice and whose good is oppression. Pray for victory. Pray for our Army, and Pray for Peace.

We must march together, all out for God. The soldier who "cracks up" does not need sympathy or comfort as much as he needs strength. We are not trying to make the best of these days. It is our job to make the most of them. Now is not the time to follow God from "afar off." This Army needs the assurance and the faith that God is with us. With prayer, we cannot fail.

Be assured that this message on prayer has the approval, the encouragement, and the enthusiastic support of the Third United States Army Commander.

With every good wish to each of you for a very Happy Christmas, and my personal congratulations for your splendid and courageous work since landing on the beach.[7]

A third version of the history of the "Fair Weather for Battle Prayer" emerged in 1960 when an Episcopal chaplain, George R. Metcalf, published *With Cross and Shovel*, his memoirs of his service in World War II. Metcalf joined Third Army headquarters in November 1944 as assistant Third Army chaplain, serving as O'Neill's executive officer. Together the two managed nearly three hundred chaplains.

Metcalf immediately developed a warm and admiring relationship with his new boss, with whom he shared an office and living quarters. Although members of different churches, the two pastors shared a spiritual and military outlook. Metcalf wrote to his wife:

We have quiet evenings of prayer and meditation. Father O'Neill tells me tales of his early priesthood and army life. He reads to me from Faber, I've introduced him to George Herbert and K. T.'s Holy Cross. We discuss subjects as "was St. Thomas really rebuked by our Lord?", "How to intercede most effectively," and the "Practice of Ejaculatory Prayer." It is an altogether new and richly helpful life for me.[8]

Metcalf also disputed Colonel Harkins's account of Patton's demanding "with curses a prayer that would 'do the job.'" He also rejected Harkins's portrayal of O'Neill and himself as "unwilling chaplains reluctantly producing a military prayer contrary to their convictions." According to Metcalf, "In truth General Patton was never anything but courteous and considerate about religious matters in my presence; and the two chaplains were quite agreeable to laying any sort of human trouble before the throne of God for the Creator's disposal as he saw fit."[9]

Metcalf claims that he received a call from Patton requesting the prayer at eight o'clock one morning shortly before Christmas. Patton asked if he had any prayers for "fair weather." Low clouds were preventing Allied planes from providing air cover for the soldiers in the Ardennes. Metcalf promised that he and O'Neill would come up with something appropriate, and the two chaplains went to work.

> When Chaplain O'Neill ... heard what was wanted, he suggested that we try independently to find or adapt a suitable prayer and then compare notes. In short order, he came up with a prayer for Victory from his Missal, and I found an Anglican petition for Fair Weather from the American Book of Common Prayer. Chaplain O'Neill then directed me to combine the two, made a few changes himself, and took the final draft to General Patton.[10]

O'Neill returned smiling, recalls Metcalf, reporting that Patton was satisfied with the prayer and intended to send it out with a Christmas Greeting to every soldier in the Third Army.

The first sentence of the prayer seems to corroborate Metcalf's account, as it is identical to the first sentence of the prayer for fair weather in the Book of Common Prayer of the Episcopal Church.[11] It is unlikely that the Irish Catholic O'Neill would have turned to an

Anglican prayer book as a guide. While O'Neill's failure to mention Metcalf's contribution may seem uncharitable, it probably reflects military protocol, according to which the authorship of work prepared by a subordinate is ordinarily ascribed to his commander. And O'Neill might have been stingy with credit because Metcalf had only recently arrived at Third Army headquarters.

The 664th Engineer Topographical Company worked around the clock to reproduce 250,000 cards bearing the prayer for fair weather and Patton's Christmas greeting. The cards and Training Letter No. 5 were distributed by December 14. Two days later, the U.S. armies in Europe were engaged in the greatest battle ever fought by American forces. The outcome of that battle, and possibly of the entire Allied war effort in Europe, would turn on the weather.

Patton's adjutant, Colonel Harkins, later wrote:

> Whether it was the help of the Divine guidance asked for in the prayer or just the normal course of human events, we never knew; at any rate, on the twenty-third, the day after the prayer was issued, the weather cleared and remained perfect for about six days. Enough to allow the Allies to break the backbone of the Von Runstedt offensive and turn a temporary setback into a crushing defeat for the enemy.
>
> General Patton again called me to his office. He wore a smile from ear to ear. He said, "God damn! Look at the weather. That O'Neill sure did some potent praying. Get him up here. I want to pin a medal on him."
>
> The Chaplain came up the next day. The weather was still clear when we walked into General Patton's office. The General rose, came from behind his desk with hand outstretched and said, "Chaplain, you're the most popular man in this Headquarters. You sure stand in good with the Lord

and the soldiers." The General then pinned a Bronze Star Medal on Chaplain O'Neill.

Everyone offered congratulations and thanks and we got back to the business of killing Germans—with clear weather for battle.[12]

On Christmas Eve, Patton and Omar Bradley attended a candle-light church service in Luxembourg City, sitting in a box once used by Kaiser Wilhelm II. Patton ordered a hot turkey dinner for every soldier in the Third Army on Christmas Day. To ensure that his order was carried out, he spent the bitterly cold day driving from one unit to another. Sergeant John Mims, Patton's driver throughout the war, recalled, "We left at six o'clock in the morning. We drove all day long, from one outfit to the other. He'd stop and talk to the troops; ask them did they get their turkey, how was it, and all that." His diary entry for that day is classic Patton: It was "a clear cold Christmas, lovely weather for killing Germans, which seems a bit queer, seeing Whose birthday it is." The troops were cheerful but "I am not, because we are not going fast enough."[13]

In the spring, as the Third Army's advance continued with clear weather, Patton again thanked the Lord for good weather: "I am very grateful to the Lord for the great blessing he has heaped on me and the Third Army, not only in the success which He has granted us, but in the weather which He is now providing."[14]

CHAPTER FIFTEEN

THE LAST ENEMY

*"Is not the taps of death but the first call to
the reveille of eternal life?"*

—NOTE WRITTEN IN PATTON'S
CADET NOTEBOOK AT WEST POINT

When the war ended in Europe, Patton returned to the United States briefly to visit his family and to deliver speeches promoting war bonds for the continuing conflict in the Pacific. He wanted to attend services at the Church of Our Saviour in San Gabriel, California, where he had been baptized and confirmed: "God has been very good to me. I would like to go there and give Him my thanks."[1]

Returning to that church on his first Sunday home, Patton told the children in Sunday school, "You are the soldiers, sailors and nurses of the next war, if we don't stop wars." He visited the graves of his parents, where he laid a wreath and prayed silently. It was to be his final trip home.

Before returning to Europe, Patton visited his two daughters, Bee and Ruth Ellen, remarking casually, "Well, I guess this is goodbye. I won't be seeing you again. Take care of your little brother, and tell John and Jim [their husbands] to take care of you." Both daughters were shocked. Ruth Ellen rejected the notion that he would not be returning home alive. "Oh, come on, Daddy, it's crazy! The war is over." Patton replied, "Well, my luck has run out. Every shell that has struck near me, struck closer each time. Front-line infantrymen use up their luck a lot faster than a rear line cook. You are born with a certain amount of luck, like money in the bank, and you spend it and it's gone. It's too damned bad I wasn't killed before the fighting stopped, but I wasn't. So be it." This was the last time his children ever saw him.[2]

Beatrice Patton was staying with her daughter Ruth Ellen in Washington, D.C., when the phone rang. The caller asked to speak with the general's wife. "It's the War Department for you!" Ruth Ellen said to her mother. Beatrice arose from the desk and knowingly said, "Something has happened to your father." On December 9, 1945, Patton was returning from a pheasant hunt with his chief of staff, Major General Hobart "Hap" Gay. Sergeant Mims, his regular driver, was in the hospital, and a substitute was at the wheel. They were traveling at about thirty-five miles per hour when an army truck turned from a side road into their path. In the glancing collision, Patton was thrown against the roof and fell forward into the glass partition behind the driver's seat. His neck was broken. Paralyzed from the neck down, he was taken to a hospital in Heidelberg. "This is a helluva way to die," Patton told Gay.[3]

In the hospital, Patton's mood alternated between profanity-laced anger and black humor. "If there's any doubt in any of your Goddamn minds that I'm going to be paralyzed for the rest of my life, let's cut out all this horse-shit right now and let me die," Patton lashed out. He just as quickly changed moods, joking, "Relax, gentlemen, I'm in no condition to be a terror now." When he was informed that the hospital chaplain was there to pray by his side, Patton responded, "Well, let him get started. I guess I need it."[4] The chaplain entered, said a few prayers and Patton thanked him.

Beatrice flew to her husband's side after ordering that her children remain at home. She seemed to want her husband to herself one final time. As they visited, Patton told his wife, "I guess I wasn't good enough." She knew he was referring to his desire to die in battle, as his ancestors had done.

On December 21, Beatrice read to Patton from John Steinbeck's novel *The Red Pony*. He asked her what time it was, and when she told him, he said that he was tired and told her she should go eat dinner; they could finish the chapter when she returned. She went to the dining room, leaving her husband with the attending nurse. Beatrice's dinner was interrupted when the nurse suddenly noticed that Patton had stopped breathing. When she returned, her husband had already died.[5] The official cause of death was pulmonary edema and congestive heart failure.

General George S. Patton Jr. was buried at mid-morning on December 24, 1945, in a grave dug by German prisoners of war. He was laid next to a Third Army soldier who had been killed in combat during the Battle of the Bulge. A United Press correspondent reported:

> Patton was buried in what he himself once called "damned poor tank country and damned bad weather." But he was buried in precision-like military ceremony, touched by pomp and tendered by grief. Big generals and little soldiers were there, as were the royalty and the commoners of this tiny country from which Patton drove the Germans in that crucial battle last Christmastide.[6]

The day after his death, the *New York Times* published a tribute:

History has reached out and embraced General George Patton. His place is secure. He will be ranked in the forefront of America's greatest military leaders. The enemy who reached their judgment the hard way, so ranked him. This country, which he served so well, will honor him no less.

George Patton had a premonition he would die in battle. It is a wonder he did not, for he took chances in the heat of the fight that made even his hard-bitten soldiers shudder....

Long before the war ended, Patton was a legend. Spectacular, swaggering, pistol-packing, deeply religious and violently profane, easily moved to anger because he was first of all a fighting man, easily moved to tears, because underneath all his mannered irascibility he had a kind heart, he was a strange combination of fire and ice. Hot in battle and ruthless too, he was icy in his inflexibility of purpose. He was no mere hell-for-leather tank commander but a profound and thoughtful military student. He has been compared with Jeb Stuart, Nathan Bedford Forrest and Phil Sheridan, but he fought his battles in a bigger field than any of them. He was not a man of peace. Perhaps he would have preferred to die at the height of his fame, when his men, whom he loved, were following him with devotion. His nation will accord his memory a full measure of that devotion.[7]

Patton's headstone is the same simple white cross that marks the graves of thousands of other American soldiers buried in military cemeteries across Europe. It is inscribed:

GEORGE S. PATTON JR
GENERAL THIRD ARMY
CALIFORNIA DEC 21 1945

His gravesite was visited so often that the area surrounding it was trampled, and his body was eventually moved to its permanent location in the shadow of the memorial that overlooks the cemetery.

In the Church of Our Saviour in San Gabriel, California, the General George S. Patton Jr. Memorial Window was dedicated in October 1946. The central image is St. George slaying the dragon, and in the lower right corner Patton is pictured mounted in a tank, an Armored Force patch on his left shoulder. St. George's shield is adorned with the "A" of the Third Army patch. The window also contains the insignias of the divisions, corps, and two armies that Patton commanded. An inscription surrounding St. George is taken from the fourth chapter of the second epistle to St. Timothy:

> I have fought a good fight.
> I have finished my course.
> I have kept the faith.

While a cadet at West Point, Patton filled a notebook with thoughts, poetry, admonitions, and principles of war. In it he inscribed what became one of his guiding principles: "What then of death? Is not the taps of death but the first call to the reveille of eternal life?"[8]

APPENDICES

GENERAL GEORGE S. PATTON

OBITUARY
SATURDAY, DECEMBER 22, 1945
NEW YORK TIMES

Gen. George Smith Patton Jr. was one of the most brilliant soldiers in American history. Audacious, unorthodox and inspiring, he led his troops to great victories in North Africa, Sicily and on the Western Front. Nazi generals admitted that of all American field commanders he was the one they most feared....

His great soldierly qualities were matched by one of the most colorful personalities of his period. About him countless legends clustered—some true, some untrue, but all testifying to the firm hold he had upon the imaginations of his men.... He was the master of an unprintable brand of eloquence, yet at times he coined phrases that will live in the American Army's traditions.

"We shall attack and attack until we are exhausted, and then we shall attack again," he told his troops before the initial landings in North Africa, thereby summarizing the military creed that won victory after victory along the long road that led from Casablanca to the heart of Germany....

[I]t was as the leader of his beloved Third Army on the Western Front that General Patton staked out his strongest claims to military greatness. In ten months his armor and infantry roared through six countries—France, Belgium, Luxembourg, Germany, Czechoslovakia and Austria. It crossed the Seine, the Loire, the Moselle, the Saar, the Rhine, the Danube and a score of lesser rivers; captured more than 750,000 Nazis, and killed or disabled 500,000 others....

His best-known nickname—"Old Blood and Guts"—was one that he detested, but his men loved. "His guts and my blood," his wounded veterans used to say when they were flown back here for hospitalization. His explosive wrath and lurid vocabulary became legendary wherever American soldiers fought.

General Patton had a softer side to his nature, too. He composed two volumes of poetry, which he stipulated were not to be published until after his death. He was an intensely religious man, who liked to sing in church and who knew the Episcopal Order of Morning Prayer by heart.

He seemed fated to be the center of controversy. Again and again, when his fame and popularity were at their height, some rash statement or ill-considered deed precipitated a storm about his head. The most celebrated of these incidents, of course, was the slapping of a soldier whom he took to be a malingerer but who was actually suffering from battle fatigue in a hospital during the Sicilian campaign.

This episode resulted in widespread demands for his removal from the command of American soldiers.... General Eisenhower sharply rebuked him, but insisted that his military qualifications, loyalty and tenacity made him invaluable in the field....

PRAYER BY LIEUTENANT GENERAL G. S. PATTON JR.

Gerald Mygatt and Henry Darlington asked a number of political and military leaders—including President Roosevelt, Secretary of War Stimson, and General Eisenhower—to contribute a prayer to the Soldiers' and Sailors' Prayer Book, published by Alfred A. Knopf in 1944. In response to that request, General Patton composed this prayer for courage.

God of our Fathers, who by land and sea has ever led us to victory, please continue Your inspiring guidance in this the greatest of our conflicts.

Strengthen my soul so that the weakening instinct of self-preservation, which besets all of us in battle, shall not blind me to my duty to my own manhood, to the glory of my calling, and to my responsibility to my fellow soldiers.

Grant to our armed forces that disciplined valor and mutual confidence which insures success in war.

Let me not mourn for the men who have died fighting, but rather let me be glad that such heroes have lived.

If it be my lot to die, let me do so with courage and honor in a manner which will bring the greatest harm to the enemy, and please, O Lord, protect and guide those I shall leave behind.

Give us the victory, Lord. *Amen.*

Lieutenant General G. S. Patton Jr.
United States Army
Commanding General, Seventh Army

HEADQUARTERS THIRD UNITED STATES ARMY APO 403

GENERAL ORDERS 9   May 1945

NUMBER 98

SOLDIERS OF THE THIRD ARMY, PAST AND PRESENT

During the 281 days of incessant and victorious combat, your penetrations have advanced farther in less time than any other army in history. You have fought your way across 24 major rivers and innumerable lesser streams. You have liberated or conquered more than 82,000 square miles of territory, including 1,500 cities and towns, and some 12,000 inhabited places. Prior to the termination of active hostilities, you had captured in battle 956,000 enemy soldiers and killed or wounded at least 500,000 others. France, Belgium, Luxembourg, Germany, Austria, and Czechoslovakia bear witness to your exploits.

All men and women of the six corps and thirty-nine divisions that have at different times been members of this Army have done their duty. Each deserves credit. The enduring valor of the combat troops has been paralleled and made possible by the often unpublicized activities of the supply, administrative, and medical services of this Army and of the Communications Zone troops supporting it. Nor should we forget our comrades of the other armies and of the Air Force, particularly of the XIX Tactical Air Command, by whose side or under whose wings we have had the honor to fight.

In proudly contemplating our achievements, let us never forget our heroic dead whose graves mark the course of our victorious advances, nor our wounded whose sacrifices aided so much in our success.

I should be both ungrateful and wanting in candor if I failed to acknowledge the debt we owe to our Chiefs of Staff, Generals Gaffey and Gay, and to the officers and men of the General and Special Staff Sections of Army Headquarters. Without their loyalty, intelligence, and unremitting labors, success would have been impossible.

The termination of fighting in Europe does not remove the opportunities for other outstanding and equally difficult achievements in the days which are to come. In some ways the immediate future will demand of you more fortitude than has the past because, without the inspiration of combat, you must maintain—by your dress, deportment, and efficiency—not only the prestige of the Third Army but also the honor of the United States. I have complete confidence that you will not fail.

During the course of this war I have received promotions and decorations far above and beyond my individual merit. You won them; I as your representative wear them. The one honor which is mine and mine alone is that of having commanded such an incomparable group of Americans, the record of whose fortitude, audacity, and valor will endure as long as history lasts.

G. S. PATTON, JR.,
General

ACKNOWLEDGMENTS

All books are an odd combination of the lonely and solitary discipline of writing and the invaluable assistance, support, and collaboration of a team of people. This book is no different. The idea for this work on Patton has its origins years ago when I was a young boy and my father presented me with a copy of Martin Blumenson's monumental work, *The Patton Papers*. I still recall the wonder that I felt poring over the heavy, hardcover book late at night absorbing Patton's life story from the raw energy that emanated from the man's own writings in his diaries and letters.

I would like to thank all those at Regnery History for their efforts to bring this book to life—Marji Ross and Harry Crocker who immediately grasped the appeal of a book dedicated to illustrating Patton's life by focusing on his formative and guiding principles, Mary Beth

Baker for helping to manage the process of publication, and Thomas Spence for his careful and patient copy editing.

I am also in admiration of the confidence and persistence of Mary Sue Seymour who encouraged my idea for the book. My friend Samantha Tang provided advice and assistance throughout the book's gestation, first in her role as an assistant at Pepperdine University's Payson Library and then as a trusted researcher. My good friend and former U.S. Army Ranger Eduardo Tinoco, assistant dean of the USC Library, was also invaluable in helping to track down articles and information whenever they defied the ability of mere mortals to find them—Rangers Lead the Way!

I would like to thank James Foley of Chicago, Illinois, for sharing his recollections of his uncle, Chaplain James O'Neill, who was the senior chaplain in Patton's Third Army and who was called upon by Patton to prepare his prayer for Good Weather. I also appreciate the assistance of the helpful staff of the US Army's Chaplain Museum at Fort Jackson, South Carolina, for their information on Chaplain O'Neill and also for making me aware of the role that George Reuben Metcalf, an Episcopal chaplain, also played in drafting Patton's Prayer for Fair Weather.

My brother, Kevin Keane, who shares some of Patton's own tempestuous personality, was helpful in suggesting the life-shaping events about Patton that form this book's chapters. As always my attorney and friend Stephen Breimer provided his valuable and unflappable counsel. Marc Ross also served as a valuable sounding board whenever I needed an intelligent and thoughtful second opinion on the book's manuscript. I am also appreciative to Larry Schiller and the Norman Mailer's Writers Colony for their work in encouraging all writers, and to my friend and mentor Jerry Green of the Pacific Council on International Policy for help with all my undertakings.

NOTES

PROLOGUE

1.   Robert H. Patton, *The Pattons: A Personal History of an American Family* (Crown, 1994), p. 184.
2.   Carlo D'Este, *Patton: A Genius for War* (HarperCollins, 1995), p. 260–61.

PART 1

1.   Robert H. Patton, *The Pattons: A Personal History of An American Family*, p. 120.
2.   Ibid.

CHAPTER 1

1.   According to Carlo D'Este in *Patton: A Genius for War* (p. 831), Henry T. Lee was an aide-de-camp to Major General Abner Doubleday (the inventor of baseball), who commanded a division defending the Union positions to the left of Cemetery Ridge during the third day of the Battle of Get-

tysburg. After the war Lee moved to Southern California, where he befriended George S. Patton II, the father of George S. Patton Jr. Lee related that he had witnessed the mortal wounding of Waller Tazewell Patton.

2.   Ruth Ellen Patton Totten, "My Father As I Knew Him," (unpublished manuscript) quoted in D'Este, *Patton*.
3.   Patton, *The Pattons*, pp. 29–31.
4.   D'Este, *Patton*, p. 11.
5.   Ibid.
6.   Much of the history of Hugh Mercer is adapted from Robert H. Patton's *The Pattons*, chapter 2, "To Die as I Have Lived."
7.   D'Este, *Patton*, p. 12.

CHAPTER 2

1.   Nat Read, *Don Benito Wilson: From Mountain Man to Mayor* (Angel City Press, 2008), p. 15.
2.   Ibid.
3.   Ibid., 51.

CHAPTER 3

1.   Patton, *The Pattons: A Personal History of an American Family*, p. 72.
2.   Notes on George William Patton are taken from Robert H. Patton, *The Pattons*.
3.   D'Este, *Patton: A Genius for War*, p. 62.
4.   Martin Blumenson, *The Patton Papers: 1885-1940*, Vol. I (Houghton Mifflin, 1972), p. 65.
5.   Totten, "My Father As I Knew Him."
6.   Ibid.
7.   D'Este, *Patton*, p. 64.
8.   Ibid., pp. 64–65.
9.   GSP II letter to GSP, both letters dated March 4, 1904.
10.   D'Este, *Patton*, p. 73.
11.   Blumenson, *Patton Papers: 1885 – 1940*, Vol. I, p. 101.
12.   Ibid., p. 109.
13.   Ibid., p. 112.
14.   Ibid., p. 118.
15.   Ibid., p. 129.
16.   Ibid., p. 195.

17. Ibid., p. 174.
18. Totten, "My Father As I Knew Him."
19. Ibid.
20. Ibid., quoted in D'Este, *Patton*, p. 339.
21. D'Este, Patton, p. 340.
22. Totten, "My Father As I Knew Him."
23. Blumenson, *The Patton Papers: 1885-1940*, Vol. II, pp. 882–83.

CHAPTER 4

1. Ruth Ellen Patton Totten, *The Button Box: A Daughter's Loving Memoir of Mrs. George S. Patton* (Univ. of Missouri, 2005), p. 67.
2. Blumenson, *Patton Papers: 1885 – 1940,* Vol. I, p. 181.
3. Quoted in D'Este, *Patton*, p. 117.
4. Ibid, p. 118, and see footnote 67 on p. 842.
5. Blumenson, *Patton Papers: 1885-1940*, Vol. II, p. 551.
6. D'Este, *Patton*, p. 218.
7. Ibid., p. 219.
8. D'Este, *Patton*, p. 309–10.
9. Ibid., p. 309.
10. Patton, *The Pattons*, p. 246.
11. Ruth Ellen Patton Totten, *The Button Box*, p. 331.
12. Blumenson, *Patton Papers: 1940-1945*, p. 292.

CHAPTER 5

1. Ruth Ellen Patton Totten, *The Button Box*, p. 303.
2. Patton, *The Pattons*, p. 143.
3. Ibid., p. 144.
4. Ibid., p. 144.
5. Ibid., pp. 147–48.
6. Ibid., p. 148.
7. D'Este, *Patton*, p. 162.
8. Ibid., p. 163.
9. Ibid., p. 164.
10. Ibid., p. 165.
11. Ibid., pp. 168–69.
12. Ibid., p. 164.
13. Ibid., p. 167.
14. Ibid., p. 42.

15. Ibid., p. 170.
16. Ibid., p. 173.
17. Pershing's orders were that his men were not to fire until they had been fired upon first.
18. D'Este, *Patton*, p. 173–74.
19. Blumenson, *Patton Papers: 1885 – 1940*, Vol. I, p. 363.
20. D'Este, *Patton*, p. 177.
21. Ruth Ellen Patton Totten, *The Button Box: A Daughter's Loving Memoir of Mrs. George S. Patton* (University of Missouri, 2005), p. 107.

CHAPTER 6

1. Carlo D'Este, *Patton: A Genius for War*, p.242.
2. Harry Semmes, *Portrait of Patton* (Appleton-Century-Crofts, 1955), p. 56.
3. Edward M. Coffman, *The War to End All Wars: The American Military Experience in World War I* (Oxford University Press, 1968), p. 301.
4. Blumenson, *Patton Papers: 1885 – 1940*, Vol. II, p. 610.
5. D'Este, *Patton*, p. 254.
6. Ladislas Farago, *Patton: Ordeal and Triumph* (Obolensky, 1963), p. 88.
7. D'Este, *Patton*, p. 255.
8. Patton, *The Pattons*, p. 183.
9. Farago, *Ordeal and Triumph*, p. 89.
10. George S. Patton Jr., letter to his wife, October 24, 1918.
11. George S. Patton Jr., letter to Nita Patton, October 26, 1918.
12. Farago, *Patton*, p. 91.

CHAPTER 7

1. No class in the history of West Point has produced more generals than the class of 1915. Of the 164 graduates, 59 members became general officers.
2. Dwight D. Eisenhower, *At Ease: Stories That I Tell To My Friends* (Doubleday & Co., 1967), p.109.
3. Martin Blumenson, *The Patton Papers: Vol. II: 1885-1940*, p. 788.
4. Carlo D'Este, *Patton: A Genius for War*, p. 293.
5. Eisenhower, *At Ease*, p. 170.
6. Ladislas Farago, *Patton: Ordeal and Triumph*, p. 101.
7. Fred Ayer, Jr., *Before the Colors Fade*, p. 78.
8. Blumenson, *The Patton Papers, Vol. II*, p. 784.
9. Ibid., p. 774.
10. D'Este, *Patton*, p. 300.

11. Farago, *Patton: Ordeal and Triumph*, p. 101.
12. D'Este, *Patton*, p. 299.
13. Blumenson, *The Patton Papers, Vol. II*, p. 799.
14. *Time*, "Milestones," Jan. 2, 1956.
15. D'Este, *Patton*, p. 300.
16. George S. Patton speech to the 304th Tank Brigade, September 28, 1920.
17. Blumenson, *The Patton Papers, Vol. II*, p. 961.
18. D'Este, *Patton*, p. 354.
19. Blumenson, *The Patton Papers, Vol. II*, p. 979.
20. D'Este, *Patton*, p. 354.
21. Blumenson, *The Patton Papers, Vol. II*, pp. 981–82.
22. Ibid., p. 1,000.
23. D'Este, *Patton*, p. 381.
24. Blumenson, *The Patton Papers, Vol. II*, p. 1,034. Patton and Joyce had a long social and professional relationship. Joyce was Patton's commanding officer at Fort Clark, Texas, and had presciently written in Patton's 1934 efficiency report, "I believe this officer could be counted on for great feats of leadership in war." (D'Este, *Patton*, p. 366.)
25. D'Este, *Patton*, p. 378.
26. Farago, *Patton: Ordeal and Triumph*, p. 123.

CHAPTER 8

1. D. A. Lande, *I Was With Patton*, p. 12.
2. Carlo D'Este recounts a vivid encounter between Patton and General Terry Allen in North Africa that dramatically demonstrated Patton's feeling about foxholes: "When he [Patton] discovered a series of slit trenches around the perimeter of the command post, Patton demanded: 'What the hell are those for?' Terry Allen replied that they were for protection against air attack by the Luftwaffe. 'Which one is yours?' When Allen pointed it out to him, Patton walked over, unzipped his fly, and urinated into it. 'There,' he said. 'Now try to use it.'" *Patton: A Genius for War*, p. 466.
3. Carlo D'Este, *Patton: A Genius for War*, p. 411.
4. The Green Hornet was a popular radio drama and comic book series about a masked crime fighter. Patton did not much resemble the character, but apparently the deep green color of his new uniform and his dramatic appearance was enough for the troops to make the connection with the comic book character.
5. Harry H. Semmes, *Portrait of Patton*, p. 22.

6.   D'Este, *Patton: A Genius for War*, p. 393.

7.   Blumenson, *The Patton Papers: 1940-1945*, p. 37.

8.   Ibid., p. 38.

9.   Ibid., p. 42.

10.   D'Este, *Patton: A Genius for War*, p. 396.

11.   Blumenson, *The Patton Papers: 1940-1945*, p. 66.

12.   Ibid., p. 63.

13.   Ibid., p. 66.

14.   Ibid., p. 74.

15.   Ibid., p. 62.

16.   D'Este, *Patton: A Genius for War*, p. 412.

17.   Ladislas Farago, *Patton: Ordeal and Triumph*, p. 170.

18.   Pogue, *George C. Marshall: Ordeal and Hope*, pp. 406–7.

19.   Ladislas Farago, *Patton: Ordeal and Triumph*, p. 176.

20.   Ibid., p. 177.

21.   Ibid., p. 178.

22.   Blumenson, *The Patton Papers: 1940-1945*, p. 93.

23.   Fred Ayer Jr., *Before the Colors Fade*, p. 120.

24.   Blumenson, *The Patton Papers: 1940-1945*, p. 97.

25.   George S. Patton, *War As I Knew It*, p. 5.

26.   Ibid., p. 8.

27.   D'Este notes that this was the only time during World War II that Patton ever publicly used the word "surrender" in any context. *Patton: A Genius for War*, p. 886.

28.   Blumenson, *The Patton Papers: 1940-1945*, p. 102.

29.   Patton was enchanted by the colors, people, and architecture of Casablanca, "a city which combines Hollywood and the Bible."

30.   D'Este, *Patton: A Genius for War*, p. 439.

31.   Blumenson, *The Patton Papers: 1940-1945*, p. 110.

32.   D'Este, *Patton: A Genius for War*, p. 437.

33.   Blumenson, *The Patton Papers: 1940-1945*, p. 108.

CHAPTER 9

1.   Patton was pleased to learn months later in a letter from his son that Napoleon had also crossed the Rhine at Oppenheim.

2.   Omar Bradley, *A Soldier's Story*, pp. 521–22.

3. Three weeks earlier Churchill had similarly relieved himself on the Sieg-fried Line, a defensive network Hitler had built to protect Germany from invasion.

4. Carlo D'Este, *Patton: A Genius for War*, p. 712.

5. William Kristol, "Men at War," *Weekly Standard*, January 23, 2012, Vol. 17, No. 18.

6. Martin Blumenson, *The Patton Papers: 1940-1945*, pp. 662–63.

7. D'Este, *Patton: A Genius for War*, p. 714.

8. Ibid., p. 275.

9. Blumenson, *The Patton Papers: 1940-1945*, p. 665.

10. D'Este, *Patton: A Genius for War*, p. 458.

11. Ibid., pp. 454–55.

12. Ibid., p. 446.

13. Ibid., p. 457.

14. Ibid., p. 460.

15. Richard Whitaker, "Task Force Baum and the Hammelburg Raid," *Armor*, September–October 1996, p. 21.

16. Ibid., p. 21.

17. Ibid.

18. Blumenson, *The Patton Papers: 1940-1945*, pp. 668–69.

19. Richard Baron, Major Abe Baum, and Richard Goldhurst, *Raid! The Untold Story of Patton's Secret Mission*, p. 43.

20. Blumenson, *The Patton Papers: 1940-1945*, p. 669.

21. Ibid., pp. 669–70. Also Whitaker, "Task Force Baum and the Hammelburg Raid," p. 24.

22. Blumenson, *The Patton Papers: 1940-1945*, p. 670.

23. Whitaker, "Task Force Baum and the Hammelburg Raid," p. 30.

24. Baron, Baum, and Goldhurst, *Raid*, pp. 263–66.

25. Blumenson, *The Patton Papers: 1940-1945*, p. 666.

26. Ibid.

27. John Toland, *The Last 100 Days*, p. 287.

28. Ibid.

29. "Statement of Donald B. Prell, former prisoner of the camp at Hammelburg," Indiana Military, accessed August 7, 2012, www.indianamilitary.org.

30. Blumenson, *The Patton Papers: 1940-1945*, p. 673.

31. Charles B. Odom, *General George S. Patton and Eisenhower*, pp. 70–71.

32. In *War As I Knew It*, Patton blamed Eddy and Hoge. "I intended to send one combat command of the 4th Armored, but, unfortunately, was talked

out of it by Eddy and Hoge, commanding the 4th Armored Division, so I compromised by sending one armored company and one company of armored infantry." *War As I Knew It*, p. 275.

33. Bradley, *A Soldier's Story*, p. 543.
34. Baron, Baum, and Goldhurst, *Raid*, p. 4.
35. Blumenson, *The Patton Papers: 1940-1945*, p. 675.
36. D'Este, *Patton: A Genius for War*, p. 717.
37. Blumenson, *The Patton Papers: 1940-1945*, p. 665.
38. Ibid.
39. Ibid., p. 676.
40. D'Este, *Patton: A Genius for War*, p. 717.
41. Blumenson, *The Patton Papers: 1940-1945*, p. 676.
42. Baron, Baum, and Goldhurst, *Raid*, p. 4.

CHAPTER 10

1. Patton diary entry, May 7, 1945. Quoted in Blumenson, *The Patton Papers: 1940-1945*, p. 697.
2. A detailed account of Operation Cowboy can be found in Karen Jensen, "How General Patton and Some Unlikely Allies Saved the Prized Lipizzaner Stallions," *World War II* magazine, September 18, 2009.
3. J. J. Hanlin, "The General and the Horses," *The American Legion*, February 1963.
4. Details on Patton's final days and medical treatment after his accident can be found in Ladislas Farago, *The Last Days of Patton*.

CHAPTER 11

1. Patton, *The Pattons*, p. 82.
2. Fifty-eight years after his surreptitious baptism by his Catholic nurse, Patton visited the Holy Land. At a chapel in Jerusalem on the site where Jesus is believed to have been crucified, Patton obtained a rosary for Mary Scally and had it blessed on the altar said to be on the exact spot where the cross was erected. Mary Scally was then ninety-six years old. George S. Patton Jr., *War As I Knew It*, p. 77.
3. Ibid., p. 90.
4. D'Este, *Patton*, p. 39.
5. Ibid., p. 36.
6. Quoted in Ibid.
7. Farago, *Patton: Ordeal and Triumph*, p. 54.

8. Patton, *The Pattons*, p. 105.
9. D'Este, *Patton*, p. 73.
10. Blumenson, *Patton Papers: 1885-1940*, Vol. I, p. 140.
11. Ibid., p. 158.
12. Blumenson, *Patton Papers: 1885-1940*, Vol. II, p. 878.
13. Fred Ayer Jr., *Before the Colors Fade: Portrait of a Soldier, George S. Patton Jr.* (Norman Berg, 1971), p. 101.
14. Blumenson, *Patton Papers: 1940-1945*, p. 133.
15. D'Este, *Patton*, p. 547.
16. Ibid., pp. 447–48.
17. Ibid., pp. 494–95.
18. Totten, *The Button Box*, p. 109.
19. Ibid., p. 279.

CHAPTER 12

1. Patton, *The Pattons*, p. 204.
2. Blumenson, *Patton Papers: 1885-1940*, Vol. I, pp. 863–64.
3. Blumenson, *Patton Papers: 1940-1945*, p. 119.
4. Brigadier General Geoffrey Keyes, a Catholic, was Patton's deputy commander.
5. Blumenson, *Patton Papers: 1940-1945*, p. 524.
6. Ibid., p. 545.
7. Ibid., p. 464.
8. Lucas's diary, January 10, 1945, cited in Carlo D'Este, *Patton*, p. 561.
9. Blumenson, *Patton Papers: 1940-1945*, p. 266.
10. Ibid., p. 75.
11. *Chicago Herald American*, March 31, 1953.
12. D'Este, *Patton*, p. 892.
13. Ibid., p. 603.
14. Brenton G. Wallace, *Patton and His Third Army*, pp. 150–51.
15. Author's conversation with James Foley, nephew of Chaplain O'Neill, 2008.
16. *Guideposts*, "Prayer for Fair Weather," December 11, 2008.
17. D'Este, *Patton*, p. 368.
18. Blumenson, *Patton Papers: 1940-1945*, p. 357.
19. D'Este, *Patton*, p. 412.
20. Blumenson, *Patton Papers: 1940-1945*, p. 371.

21. D. A. Lande, *I Was With Patton: First-Person Accounts of WWII in George S. Patton's Command* (Zenith, 2002), p. 177.

22. Blumenson, *Patton Papers: 1940-1945*, p. 574.

23. Ibid., p. 491.

24. Patton, *The Pattons*, p. 226.

25. D'Este, *Patton*, p. 325.

26. An important Hindu scripture. Patton's aunt had read him translations of the text when he was a boy.

27. Patton, *The Pattons*, p. 226.

28. The title comes from I Corinthians 13:12, "For now we see through a glass, darkly; but then face to face: now I know in part; but then shall I know even as also I am known."

29. Rudyard Kipling, "Recessional" (1897).

30. Kipling, "Hymn Before Action" (1896).

31. Blumenson, *Patton Papers: 1940-1945*, p. 187.

32. Ibid., p. 357.

33. Ibid., p. 268.

34. Ibid., p. 256.

35. Ibid., p. 859.

36. Ibid., p. 503.

37. Lande, *I Was With Patton*, p. 290.

38. The wife of Henry Luce, publisher of *Time* and *Life*, Clare Boothe Luce (1903–1987) served in Congress (Republican, Connecticut, from 1943 to 1947) and as ambassador to Italy (1953 to 1956).

39. Lande, *I Was With Patton*, p. 177.

40. Blumenson, *Patton Papers: 1940-1945*, p. 312.

41. Brigadier General Geoffrey Keyes, Patton's deputy commander, who was Roman Catholic.

42. Blumenson, *Patton Papers: 1940-1945*, p. 303.

43. Kay Summersby Morgan, *Past Forgetting: My Love Affair with Dwight D. Eisenhower* (Simon and Schuster, 1976), pp. 165–66.

44. Roger Nye, *The Patton Mind* (Avery, 1993), p. 162.

45. Patton, *The Pattons*, p. 197.

46. Ibid.

CHAPTER 13

1. D'Este, *Patton*, p. 588.

2. Letter from Dwight D. Eisenhower to George S. Patton Jr., April 29, 1944, in Alfred D. Chandler et al., *The Papers of Dwight David Eisenhower,* Vol. I, pp. 1839–40.

3. Blumenson, *The Patton Papers: 1940-1945,* p. 451.

4. "Overlord" was the code name for the coming Allied invasion of Nazi-occupied Europe, which would begin on June 6, 1944—D-Day—in Normandy.

5. Privately in a letter to his wife, Beatrice, Patton would write much less charitably of English women: "If there were ever any pretty women in England, they must have died. They are hideous, with fat ankles." Martin Blumenson, *The Patton Papers: 1940-1945,* p. 82.

6. D'Este, *Patton,* p. 586.

7. That same day Patton offered to have his name withdrawn from the list in order not to jeopardize the promotion of others.

8. Ibid., p. 583.

9. Blumenson, *The Patton Papers: 1940-1945,* p. 326.

10. Ibid., p. 197.

11. Patton, *The Pattons,* pp. 257–58.

12. Totten, *The Button Box,* p. 161.

13. Blumenson, *The Patton Papers: 1940-1945,* p. 315.

14. Charles R. Codman, *Drive* (Little, Brown, 1957), p. 111.

15. Allan Carpenter, *George Smith Patton, Jr.: The Last Romantic* (Vero Beach, FL, 1987), p. 79.

16. D'Este, *Patton,* p. 538.

17. Blumenson, *The Patton Papers: 1940-1945,* p. 315.

18. "Patton and Truth," *Time,* December 6, 1943.

19. Patton, *The Pattons,* p. 175.

20. Ibid., pp. 179–80.

21. William Manchester, *American Caesar: Douglas MacArthur: 1880-1964* (Boston, 1978), p. 115.

22. Patton, *The Pattons,* p. 202.

23. Phillip Knightley, *The First Casualty* (Harcourt Brace Jovanovich, 1975), pp. 320–21.

24. "Patton and Truth," *Time.*

25. Pearson later played a prominent role in the downfall of Secretary of Defense James V. Forrestal by questioning his mental stability. President

Truman dismissed Forrestal, who eventually fell to his death from a sixteenth-floor window at Bethesda Naval Hospital.

26. Blumenson, *The Patton Papers: 1940-1945*, p. 377.

27. Ibid., p. 380.

28. Dwight D. Eisenhower, *Crusade in Europe* (Doubleday, 1948), p. 201.

29. Blumenson, *The Patton Papers: 1940-1945*, p. 381.

30. Patton, *The Pattons*, p. 185. The actual text of I Cor. 15:26 reads, "The last enemy that shall be destroyed is death."

31. Blumenson, *The Patton Papers: 1885-1940*, Vol. I, p. 17, and Judges 15:14–17.

32. Blumenson, *The Patton Papers: 1940-1945*, p. 377–78.

33. Ibid., p. 378.

34. Ibid., p. 382.

35. George S. Patton Jr., *War as I Knew It* (Houghton Mifflin, 1947), p. 76–78.

36. Ibid., pp. 84–86.

37. Blumenson, *Patton Papers: 1940-1945*, p. 397.

38. D'Este, *Patton*, p. 600.

39. Ibid., p. 593.

40. Blumenson, *Patton Papers: 1940-1945*, p. 477.

41. Ibid., p. 480.

CHAPTER 14

1. Harold A. Winters *et al.*, *Battling the Elements: Weather and Terrain in the Conduct of War* (Johns Hopkins Univ. Press, 2001), p. 29.

2. Blumenson, *Patton Papers: 1940-1945*, p. 570.

3. V. E. Friedenwald Jr. and C. Crossen, "Vascular Anastomosis," *Scientific American, Science and Medicine,* Vol. 1, No. 4, September-October 1994, pp. 68–77.

4. Alexis Carrel, *The Voyage to Lourdes* (Harper & Row, 1939).

5. Reverend Stanley Jaki, "Two Lourdes Miracles and a Nobel Laureate: What Really Happened?" address to the Catholic Medical Association, 1998, http://www.catholicculture.org/culture/library/view.cfm?id=286 6&CFID=132716071&CFTOKEN=51997166.

6. Ibid.

7. James H. O'Neill, "The True Story of the Patton Prayers," *The Military Chaplain* 19, no. 2 (October – November 1948), p. 3.

8. George R. Metcalf, *With Cross and Shovel* (Riverside Press, 1960), p. 176.

9. Ibid., p. 185.

10. Ibid., p. 184.

11. The prayer "For Fair Weather" from the 1928 Book of Common Prayer reads, "Almighty and most merciful Father, we humbly beseech thee, of thy great goodness, to restrain those immoderate rains, wherewith thou hast afflicted us. And we pray thee to send us such seasonable weather, that the earth may, in due time, yield her increase for our use and benefit; through Jesus Christ our Lord. Amen."

12. George S. Patton Jr., *War As I Knew It*, pp. 185–86.

13. D'Este, *Patton*, p. 691.

14. Blumenson, *The Patton Papers: 1940-1945*, p. 659.

CHAPTER 15

1. D'Este, *Patton*, p. 748.

2. Ibid., p. 750.

3. Totten, *The Button Box*, p. 350.

4. D'Este, *Patton*, p. 788.

5. Totten, *The Button Box*, p. 351.

6. D'Este, *Patton*, p. 802.

7. Ibid., pp. 803–4.

8. Ibid., p. 87.

INDEX

251